BREEDING DOGS
A Practical Guide

BREEDING DOGS

A Practical Guide

Patsy Hollings and Stephen Hollings

THE CROWOOD PRESS

First published in 2011 by
The Crowood Press Ltd
Ramsbury, Marlborough
Wiltshire SN8 2HR

www.crowood.com

British Library Cataloguing-in-Publication Data
A catalogue record for this book is available from the British Library.

ISBN 978 1 84797 257 6

The author and the publisher do not accept any responsibility in any manner whatsoever for any error or omission, or any loss, damage, injury, adverse outcome, or liability incurred as a result of the use of any of the information contained in this book, or reliance upon it. This book is not in any way intended to replace, or sidestep, the veterinary surgeon, and with regard to any aspect of their dog's health, readers should seek professional advice from a veterinary surgeon.

Acknowledgments
Our grateful thanks go to the Kennel Club; Caroline Kisko; Helen Davenport; Emma Smith BVMS (Hons) MRCVS, who took the time to advise on Chapter 3; Andrew Brace and Zena Thorn-Andrews, for contributing photos of their excellent dogs. Thanks also to the professionals, the amazing Lisa Croft-Elliott, Carol Ann Johnson, Sally Anne Thompson, and of course Peter Barber, who was always there to deal with my whims and wants – the pictorial side of this book would not have been so brilliantly expressive without Peter. Thank you to all who let us take photographs of your dogs and use them in this book.

Photographs by Peter Barber except where credited otherwise.
Illustrations by Caroline Pratt.

Typeset by Jean Cussons Typesetting, Diss, Norfolk
Printed and bound in Singapore by Craft Print International

CONTENTS

PREFACE

THE IMPORTANCE OF RESPONSIBLE BREEDING

Mating dogs is not dog breeding; it is the reproduction of dogs.

A breeder should be seeking to mate the right dogs in the right way so that he produces the ideal (or as near to it as possible) in his kennels.

That is only feasible if the breeder knows what the ideal is.

Dr Malcolm Willis, BSc, PhD

This book is designed to help dog breeders breed healthy, happy dogs which can live long, contented lives within a family environment, and enable you, the breeder, to educate and support new buyers. In our view a pedigree dog has the advantage over the crossbred dog because his breed characteristics and temperament can be researched by new dog owners. Furthermore the Kennel Club (KC) can advise new dog owners as to the good, responsible breeders who

Helen Davenport-Willis is a conscientious breeder of the Bernese Mountain Dog, seen here with her home-bred champion Nellsbern Valentino. (Photo: Ian Anderson)

will have observed the necessary health-screening programmes for heritable conditions.

It is important to be aware that a dog is quite different from other 'pets'. A cat is primarily independent, so does not require the same commitment from his owners, nor is he strong enough to cause them any physical problems; birds and small caged rabbits and rodents fall into the same category. If the family has a horse and he is difficult, he lives in a field and stable and there is no need for them to have particularly close contact with him. A dog, on the other hand, is protective of his 'pack', he lives within the family home, much as a family member, and consequently if he is not sound in body or mind, or indeed brought up with knowledge and informed training, he can become a danger to family members or anyone within his social environment.

The Akita is a strong dog that will not be aggressive towards humans if trained correctly, but it will protect the family.

By way of comparison, when you buy a car, you will be careful to look to a reputable dealer for advice as to which make of car will best fit your needs. You will require a warranty, an honest dealership, and a suitable brand at a cost that reflects your budget. If these are not the criteria you look for when you buy your car, then perhaps you opt to buy something cheap and cheerful from some unscrupulous cheapjack dealer – but if you do this, the car you end up with could be unroadworthy and put your family in danger.

So do you want to breed dogs and gain a reputation for excellence, or would you simply 'puppy farm', with no respect for the welfare of either people or dogs, and where the only motivating factor is money? This latter policy risks exposing the families to whom you sell your puppies to potentially serious problems as a result of their lack of knowledge concerning rearing and training, and the dog at best having to be rehomed, which could mean him having to spend months in kennels, or at worst being put to sleep. Remember, the puppy did not ask to be born: he is your responsibility.

Both of us are from a farming background; we are steeped in country ways, and hope our no-nonsense Yorkshire origins will make you think about why you want to breed dogs. I don't want to put you off dog breeding: through our dogs we have had the opportunity to learn, to follow a thoroughly fulfilling vocation, and ultimately to meet like-minded people from the world over. This has brought a sense of fulfilment to our lives, especially when we receive emails, letters and calls from people who say their dog has brought enormous pleasure to their own lives, whether he is a family pet, a working companion or a top show dog.

1 THE RESPONSIBILITIES OF BREEDING

For over 20,000 years man and dog have worked together. Initially man 'harnessed' the wolf to help the future of his race, in that the wolf would kill prey for itself and the human would scavenge the kill to eat. As time went by the partnership between wolf and man developed: with the tools he was able to make, the human could bring the kill to a close more easily, but he needed the wolf's sense of smell and speed to flush out the game. The man would then be the first to take his fill of the more easily available meat from the carcase, and the wolf would have the remains, its powerful jaws able to extract morsels that the man couldn't get to. This arrangement determined that the man was the 'leader of the pack', and this philosophy persists today – or it should if dog and man are to live with mutual respect: man should *always* be higher in the pecking order.

SO WHY BREED PEDIGREE DOGS?

Every breed of dog was developed for a specific purpose, some for finding, hunting, flushing and retrieving game, others to protect the home and domestic stock, and finally small dogs as playmates and companions. Herding dogs were developed so that domestic animals could be gathered more quickly and easily, guard dogs were bred specifically to look after

This Pointer is using both nose and tail to display evidence of scent, thus performing her natural instinct, pointing game for her master.

the family and homestead, and terriers to go to ground and keep the family environment free from vermin. As man's knowledge and the bounds of civilization increased, so too did the efficacy of his partnership with the dog, and today we continue to benefit from the dog's role of servitude to mankind, in the following ways:

- As a companion: it is a known fact that people who have dogs live longer, less stressful lives. The world we live in increasingly causes us stress, with deadlines, rushing to travel on crowded trains and motorways. Just walking the dog or sitting stroking him lowers blood pressure and heart rate, and modifies respiration. And for those who are overtly lonely, having a dog to interact with is wholly beneficial to their wellbeing; furthermore, when you take the dog for a walk, people will often stop and chat, which rarely happens to those walking alone, who are often viewed with suspicion.
- As a workmate to farmers – even though technology has advanced to the countryside in that cows can now be completely managed by robots, which let them into the parlour, feed and milk them, and grade the milk, sending it to the bulk tank or the waste bucket: amazing! But the sheepdog is needed to herd youngstock and sheep.
- For sport and recreation, such as agility competitions, showing, field trialling, Young Kennel Club events.
- For man's health and wellbeing: guide dogs are supremely acknowledged for their service to mankind, giving independence to people otherwise dependent on others. 'Hearing' dogs work in a similar way, and are trained

ABOVE: Much pleasure and many health benefits are to be gained by just stroking your dog.

BELOW: The farmer surveys his land with his loyal sheepdogs.

to alert their handler in times of need. Dogs for the disabled can, for example, load the washing machine, being that essential extra pair of hands. PAT dogs go into hospitals and hospices, giving comfort to the sick or lonely.

- As 'sniffer' dogs, trained to detect drugs, or to hunt for people who are lost, sometimes for the police or in the snow, or on mountains, trying to locate walkers who are lost. Other important work is with the police or the army, in detaining criminals, or detecting drugs or bombs.
- In detecting cancer: this is a relatively new procedure, but is vital in identifying the disease in its early stages.

For some people dogs provide security, or perhaps an interest in life, and they are used in many aspects of recreation, such as dog showing, field trials, agility, obedience, to name just a few. All of these contribute to making dogs an invaluable and integral part of society.

PEDIGREE VERSUS CROSSBREED

Many dogs, both pedigree and crossbreed, are used in the categories described above – so what are the advantages of breeding the pedigree? Actually the term 'pedigree dog' is used to determine that a dog has typical traits that are consistent with a pure breed, and a lineage that can be made known to fanciers of the breed so that the type, and the soundness of body and mind can be built on, health can be monitored, and permanent identification can control the individual breed's welfare, managed by the Kennel Club (KC).

However, all dogs have pedigrees, it is just that the ancestry of the crossbreed is not known, as records are not kept. It

could be averred that many crossbreed dogs are bred irresponsibly – which might be right, however it must be said that not all purebred dogs are necessarily healthy and sound, for two main reasons: first, not every dog breeder has impeccable ethics; and second, we are working with nature, which inevitably sets us limits. To build a car or a ten-storey building we can be trained explicitly to perfect such an amazing feat; however, when working with living beings, not all is predictable, or can even be explained. We can do every diagnostic health test imaginable, study genetics, prepare, and cover every angle – but Nature will sometimes just tap us on the shoulder and remind us that she has the last word. This is all the more reason only to embark on breeding programmes where as much information as possible is available to us – hence the 'pedigree dog'.

The Crossbreed Dog
And so we pass to the crossbreed dog. Although many crossbreeds could be said to be irresponsibly bred, this is not true of

This Lurcher is a crossbred dog, produced with thought by enthusiasts for speed and hunting ability.

ABOVE: The hunt terrier is bred to go to ground, and as such must be brave and quick-thinking. Although not recognized by the Kennel Club, he is bred with knowledge and care.

BELOW: Foxhounds working with the hunt are instinctive and live happily in a pack.

all of them, by any means. Many dogs bred for a specific purpose are not registered by the KC, as, for example, Lurchers, which are bred with a great knowledge of the lines used. Sometimes their breeders would say they only breed for instinct, but if you investigate a little more and talk at greater length with the breeders of these dogs, the conversation will reveal how they choose the sire of the litter – they might use a greyhound type for speed, and then breed the resulting puppy back to the rough-haired great-grandsire, thus line breeding on instinct.

Similar formats are used by stockmen who produce hunt terriers. Obviously the resulting puppies bred in this way have to be sound, and again this is done on instinct. The bottom line is that this breeding is done for a valid reason, and not through carelessness or for direct monetary gain.

There are also breeds that are bred for a purpose and not registered by the KC: the Jack Russell Terrier, working sheepdogs, working foxhounds, racing greyhounds. These breeds are regulated by their relevant affiliated institute: the British Jack Russell Terrier Club (BJRTC), the Greyhound Stud Book (GSB), the International Sheepdog Society (ISDS), the Master of Foxhounds Association (MFHA), the Masters of Harriers and Beagles Association (MHBA), the National Greyhound Racing Club (NGRC). Also dogs may be registered with the Guernsey Kennel Club (GKC) and the Kennel Club of Jersey (KCJ). Dogs registered with another organization within the British Isles, and recognized by the Kennel Club, may be accepted for registration on the breed register on submission of documented evidence, including the pedigree, from the appropriate organization.

Dogs can also be imported from abroad and registered with the KC, provided they are registered with their own country's kennel club, and that it is recognized by the KC. An imported dog will have a suffix after its name, IMP, so will be instantly recognizable as an imported dog. The introduction of the pet passport has made it far easier to travel abroad with your dog, perhaps to a dog show or to mate your bitch, thereby widening boundaries and broadening gene pools. Nevertheless it is wise to consult the KC before embarking on such procedures to make sure you are cognisant of the current regulations, otherwise you may not be able to register the puppies.

Often, areas within the media and animal-related organizations would have the public believe that the irresponsibly bred crossbreed is healthy and should be the choice of pet above the pedigree dog, the implication being that the pedigree dog is bred by fanciers who show the breed of choice purely for how the dog looks. Type is of paramount importance when breeding carefully, and so line breeding is essential – the total outcross will not produce dogs of the correct look, or, more importantly, of the required temperament: temperament is confirmed by line breeding, through condensing the lines (*see Chapter 3*). The media also brings human ethics into the equation, thereby inferring that any line breeding is unacceptable; however, weren't Adam and Eve responsible for the start of human evolution? Interbreeding is followed by most stockmen in order to condense the positives in their stock, giving stronger, healthier animals which can fulfil their purpose with less effort and stress.

Although crossbreeds can have the advantage of hybrid vigour, in fact if you think about it, the dog which roams the street looking for a mate will quite probably copulate with a close relative, due to locality. How many urchin dogs pack their bag and catch a train to look for a mate that is totally unrelated!

If a litter is produced by mistake because someone was not vigilant when the bitch was in season, the puppy's ancestry will be unknown: who was sire? What traits will the puppy develop? How big will the offspring grow? Are there hereditary defects, physical or of temperament, in the pedigree? None of these questions can be answered, so no support can be given.

These puppies are probably advertised as available either by word of mouth, or in the local free ads or in the pet shop window, and very often as free to a good home. And if a price is asked for them, it will probably be for relatively little, so potential owners will think the puppy is a bargain (much like the car from the back-street dealer). Furthermore the new owners might not have fully thought through the implications of this addition to the family, and might have acquired the puppy on impulse; and without any firm commitment the puppy will be at risk of not being reared with knowledge and perseverance.

As the puppy grows into adolescence, his potentially unsociable behaviour – chewing things, being defiant, possibly even wanting to take control – may lead to him being abandoned or put in a rescue centre. As a crossbreed, no breed-specific rescue service is available. If he is lucky he will end up in a national rescue centre, where he will have to wait until it is to be hoped someone will take pity on him. Each registered breed has a rescue midpoint, where dedicated, well-informed volunteers give in-depth information on the idiosyncrasies of that particular breed to the prospective home before a dog is placed in it, giving him the best possible chance of a successful rehoming.

Designer Dogs

There is a new trend developing of breeding 'designer dogs', and this practice can be worrying for dependable dog breeders, since putting together different breeds of dog is not perpetuating awareness of how the puppy will grow or the hereditary issues that could evolve. Mixing a terrier with a gundog could breed the swift bite to kill of a terrier on a rat with the size and strength of a gundog, with the potential for frightening consequences. Most pure-bred dogs have been specifically bred for their purpose over hundreds of years by real grassroots stockmen, and right up to

A typical Ladradoodle.

present day requirements by dedicated fanciers.

Why is there any need to cross these carefully developed breeds, if not for money? Surf the Internet and it can be seen that designer dogs are promoted like designer handbags, which is scary. Is the incentive to acquire these breeds based on fashion? Surely this is not the way to choose a puppy. It seems that certain celebrities seek out these dogs because they compliment their designer lifestyle – but just as clothes go out of fashion, what happens when these dogs go out of style? So many of these crosses are advertised, from Labradoodles (a cross between a Labrador and a Poodle), Beacols (a Beagle/Bearded Collie cross) – and so on, too many to mention. Some will say this is progress, and perhaps the dedicated are right in their thinking; but they could be in the minority, and what is the motivation in these cases, and at what cost to the dog?

WHY BREED?

This question can be answered with honest respect by breeders of pedigree dogs. If done with calm logic and a passion for the pure-bred dog, the breed will go forwards, enhancing the dog's life and the family who researched the breed, and the breeder who can offer support and communication for the whole of the dog's life, if necessary. Speaking to good breeders, each will have a tale of someone who has contacted them to say they have lost their much-loved pet at a grand old age, leaving the said owner devastated; but this is one of the main reasons that makes dog breeding so worthwhile.

Dog Breeding by Chance

A great many people choose the breed of dog that appeals to them, and fall into dog breeding almost by chance. Having chosen a well bred dog they feel they would like to put its abilities to good use, often by showing it, but maybe also by working it in agility classes or as a gundog or tracking dog. Because they enjoy exploiting the dog's ability, and also the social element of integration with like-minded people, the natural progression is to want to breed from the dog they have, and to use a puppy they have bred in future events. It is also extremely rewarding to breed a dog that can win with an owner who is just starting out, and seeing the relationship between the pair develop.

Before you embark on any breeding programme, however, you need to take a careful look at your dog. Take off the rose-tinted glasses: everyone believes he has the finest dog, in the same way that everyone has the greatest child or partner, but it is essential to be objective and to ask yourself if he truly has the quality

Breeding a good dog is rewarding; the aim should be to improve with each litter, retaining the soundness and qualities of the ancestors, thus making it rewarding when puppy and parent share the same traits.

The Averis Family with a selection of their world famous terriers; the mutual devotion is evident and contributes to the continued success of the kennel. (Photo: Judy Averis)

to take the breed forwards. Nor should you be in a hurry; a lot can be gained if you simply watch and learn from experienced dog people who have a reputation for excellence. You may feel that they are unapproachable – remember, anything competitive can ignite jealousy, and experienced dog folk have effectively been there and done it, and don't tend to be hanging around chatting: it is often the less successful who are there gossiping about the successful.

Besides, if something is worth doing, it's worth doing well. So don't be afraid to ask for advice, but courteously enquire of someone you respect as to when would be the best time to talk about the breed, as you want to learn – we've all had to start at some time. Dedicated folk will be happy and able to help; they may recommend that you visit at home, where they would have time to chat without distractions. Endeavour to visit in the more relaxed environment of their home: with good dogs all around, you can learn so much, and can certainly learn to appreciate the good points of the breed. I have always loved just listening to the tales told by older dog men – especially terrier folk, who tell it like it is and entertain with their stories, which although perhaps are sometimes a little exaggerated, are mostly based in sound knowledge.

The Showman Breeder

In the world of dog showing, the enthusiastic newcomer often finds himself falling victim to the following scenario:

Man gets a puppy and starts to show him; he wins a little, and so man becomes increasingly enthusiastic. Man meets like-minded people who give guidance on how to get the best from the puppy in the show ring. Camaraderie develops, and showing becomes a big part of the social life of dog and owner. Two years pass, and man decides to breed from his dog, so uses his friend's dog as the sire. The resulting puppies are so wonderful that he can't settle on which to keep to show, so he keeps two; these puppies are trained to within an inch of their lives and so perform well in the ring, where they gain limited success.

Another two years pass and puppies have grown up, perhaps not fulfilling early expectations, so the dam is bred again, this time to the winning dog of the moment. Again two puppies are retained: they are so superb that decisions are hard to make. Man now has five dogs, all under the age of five..... Five years on and man has five old dogs.

This type of breeder is ignorant of his responsibility to the dog, and it is to be hoped that he is among those reading this book.

The Puppy Farmer

There is another sort of breeder, namely the puppy farmer. Furthermore there are two types of puppy farmer: first, the farmer who can no longer make a living following traditional farming methods (milking cows, rearing pigs for meat or sheep for wool). Government grants were given to these struggling farmers, mainly situated in Wales, to help them diversify into other ways of utilizing their natural skills and land, and some of these thought that breeding dogs would earn a good living. The skill these farmers lacked was in educating new owners as to the needs of the breed of dog they were producing. As farmers they would make a good job of rearing their normal farm stock: the animals would have a stress-free life, and therefore grow healthy, strong, happy and fit for purpose, whether making milk, or to sell or fatten for the table. In this world, however, temperament or long-term health screening was not an issue, as it should be with the pet that lives integrally within the family.

The other type of puppy farmer is quite unscrupulous in his desire just to make as much money as he can, rather like the cheapjack dealer who sells cheap rather than safe cars. But whereas the car can be scrapped if it is dangerous, the life of a badly bred dog is our responsibility, and we at least owe him a future. Moreover these bad breeders will breed from a bitch each time she comes in season, they will probably not feed or worm either bitch or puppies correctly, nor will they have organized pre-booked homes, and so will probably sell the litter to some pet supermarket, often with pedigrees that are not applicable to the puppies. This practice serves to imply to a new owner that a puppy bought 'off the shelf' can be just as easily discarded, much as one would discard an outfit that falls out of fashion. In fact such shops have often sold puppies to celebrities, whose photographs are then displayed around the reception area: to devoted dog people the implications of this practice are quite alarming.

Puppies used as a commodity in this way are often sick due to lack of husbandry, and the fact that, although the kennel area appears clean, the number of puppies coming and going makes it impossible to keep the kennel free of germs and infections. Those vets whose practice embraces these supermarkets will straightaway be able to identify a puppy bought from these outlets.

At risk of appearing cynical, these instances show how important it is to observe good dog-breeding practice.

THE IMPORTANCE OF SHOWING

Dog showing is an aid to breeding good dogs: the progeny produced by a certain sire can be seen at first hand and its qualities assessed, without having to rely on hearsay or the acclaim of the dog's owner. I have heard the owner of a certain male dog exclaim that it should be avoided in the show ring that day 'because he is in a bad mood'. Well, that male was in a bad mood for all of the five years that he was shown, and funnily enough he often produced progeny that were also often in a bad mood.

The judge plays an important part in the future of the dogs he judges; thus a knowledgeable judge will consider type, balance, health, soundness, temperament and quality in equal parts, without fear or favour. An inexperienced judge who is full of his own importance can have clouded judgement, putting up a dog to win because he is friendly with its handler, or even putting a dog which has won great accolades to a lower placing,

When judging, the judge is looking for soundness and health – these attributes will always be found in dogs that win. (Photo: Lisa Croft-Elliott)

trying to prove that he knows more and can find a better dog than all the more experienced judges. So those embarking on a judging career should remember that the dogs judged would be recognized as quality animals, and so they have a responsibility to the future of the breed and the dogs they are judging.

If you want to include a dog in your family and/or commence dog breeding it is advisable that first of all you should contact the Kennel Club.

THE KENNEL CLUB

The Kennel Club is the governing body, and the UK's largest organization committed to the well-being, good health and care of dogs.

The chairman of the Kennel Club is an active and knowledgeable dog man, seen here with wife Kate assessing the quality of a Border Terrier.

The national show of sporting and other dogs, now known as 'The National' and run by Birmingham Dog Show Society, is the world's oldest surviving dog show: the first show by this society was in 1859. The motivation for the creation of dog shows, was, as indeed it is now, to compare one dog against another, and the winner will be the one who excelled in type, soundness, temperament, showmanship and that indefinable trait, quality. Lords of the manor, farmers, gamekeepers and the like would love to show off their stock as the best, ultimately their dogs.

The twelve men who were the committee of the National Dog Club, gathered together and headed by Mr S. E. Shirley, MP, formed the Kennel Club, and the meeting was held on 4 April 1873 at 2 Albert Mansions, Victoria Street, London. Thus the Kennel Club came into being.

The Kennel Club introduced the first volume of the studbook, which to this day lists all dogs that have won an award, thereby qualifying inclusion. Mr Frank C. S. Pearce, son of the Rev. Thomas Pearce, of the renowned 'Idstone' kennel was the studbook's first editor, and also contributed to *The Field* magazine. This

This was the form issued by the Kennel Club in 1974, granting our affix.

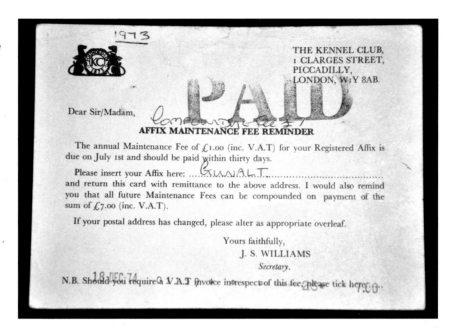

first volume had records of shows from 1859 to 1873, in which year a calendar was introduced recording events, for the first ten years listing two shows each year.

The first organized dog show, controlled by Messrs Shorthouse and Page, was in Newcastle-upon-Tyne on 28–29 June 1859, and consisted of sixty entries from setter and pointer breeds. The dogs were entered by their kennel name – early catalogue entries read Mr Murrel's 'Spot' and Mr Brown's 'Venus' – as specific breed classes were not justified at this time, so they would compete in the same class together. The winner would be awarded prize money of 22s (wish it were that much today!)

Obviously some sort of structure needed to be put in place, since Spot, Rex and Fly were the common names for many dogs. So in 1880 the KC introduced a 'universal registration' of dog names, which was viewed with suspicion at first, as are most 'new' systems. At this early stage of dog shows the registration of the dog's name was the important feature in the stud book, as pedigrees were not considered important at this point. Over the next few years, new rules and regulations were created, forming a sound system of government that has subsequently been adopted by kennel clubs throughout the world.

Recognized breeders now have an affix, applicable only to that kennel owner, making it easy to see at a glance the breeder of a particular strain within breeds. All dogs owned and bred by us, for instance, will bear the 'Gunalt' affix, and if we obtain a dog from a different line we can add the affix to the *end* of the dog's name, which shows that we did not breed the dog. Anyone owning a bitch that we have bred, and mating it to a sire that we bred, cannot add our affix. We applied for our affix in 1973, and in 1974 were able to compound our affix for life for a fee of £7: fortunately we took advantage of this facility – had we not, we would now have to pay an annual fee. This ruling was introduced because many people would start off enthusiastically showing and breeding, but after a few years would leave in pursuit of other interests, which meant that the KC were amassing affixes that were dormant. The annual fee put a stop to this, however.

Dog showing is a social, competitive, participant activity, which stimulated people's interest; hence it caught the attention of many, and increasingly women – and even members of the royal family. For example, HRH the Prince of Wales greatly supported the movement to eradicate the practice of cropping dogs' ears, and from 9 April 1898, dogs with cropped ears were not eligible to compete in Kennel Club licensed events.

By 1900, nearly thirty championship shows were licensed, and minor shows were on the increase. It was the policy of the committee to keep the regulations to a minimum, so shows were 'recognized, 'licensed' or 'sanctioned' if the executive of the show agreed to adopt the KC show regulations. Thus guarantors of the show signed an undertaking, and still do, to hold and conduct the show in accordance with the rules and regulations of the KC. By 2004, 3,926 licences were issued for various canine activities, 1,048 of which were companion shows.

The total number of dogs registered by the KC in 1967 was 146,046; in 2007 this number had increased to, 270,707, show-

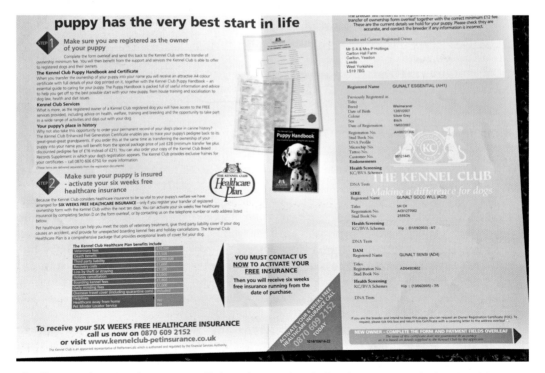

The litter registration form states all the relevant details for the puppy, including health-screening results.

Showing develops mutual respect in both the dog and its young handler; as an activity, it also gives young people a social focus.

ing the interest in pure-bred dogs for pets, showing, demonstration and other KC-registered events. In 1981, the KC came into the twentieth century and became computerized; this made registrations of litters quicker, easier to record and trace, thus keeping mistakes to a minimum.

By putting data on the central computer it is easy to record health data on individual dogs and breeds. The KC works tirelessly in the promotion of health and the careful breeding of dogs, and has a strong relationship with the British Veterinary Association (BVA). The KC introduced the recording of hip dysplasia data in 1965, and in the last twenty years alone over 100,000 x-rays have been assessed, with the results contained on the KC database. Other health screenings include eye testing, and elbow dysphasia testing.

The KC has also introduced the KC Charitable Trust, with many breed clubs instrumental in the funding of DNA testing. Through DNA records, breeders can assess the incidence of inherited diseases, accordingly helping to breed fitter dogs, several generations further on.

In this day of media hype and anti-dog legislation, the KC has diversified from just the care of the pure-bred dog, introducing the canine code in 1988, and furthering accountability with the good citizen dog scheme, designed at educating people towards responsible dog ownership in 1992.

Always forward thinking, the KC went another step forwards when in 1985 the Young Kennel Club (the YKC) was instigated. What a future afforded to the young, teaching growing juveniles the importance of respect for others, human and animal, giving a purpose and confidence invaluable for their future. In my youth I was a member of the Young Farmers Club, and both these organizations provide alternatives to standing on street corners, looking for mischief. Moreover, as breeders we need to make sure that the dogs we breed are of sufficiently good soundness and temperament that YKC members can enjoy a long, happy time with their dogs.

Amongst the educational events offered by the KC is the successful 'Discover Dogs', which helps people to make informed and responsible choices on choosing the most suitable breed for them. Thus each breed club has a stand with exhibits of that particular breed, and members of the public can speak at leisure to representatives who will also enlighten them as to the characteristics of that particular breed.

Of course the most notable event, and the one the public identifies the KC with, is Crufts dog show, the largest dog show in the world and witnessed by people the world over. Crufts 2008 was held at the National Exhibition Centre, Birmingham, from 6–9 March: over 160,000 attended, to see an entry of 22,948 dogs compete over the four days.

Many like to look for negatives within the KC, and any high profile organization is open to criticism; however, I liken the KC to one's parents, in that we can afford to react against them because we know they are there for us, but without them we would flounder. The KC constantly strives for the good of all dogs, and all moneys accrued are ploughed back into the KC for the benefit of all dogs.

(For further information about the KC, go to their website – *see* page 189.)

IN SUMMARY

To sum up this chapter, all dogs can be of great benefit to the human race, whether crossbreed or pedigree, but the advantage of the purebred dog that is registered with the Kennel Club, when bred with prudence, honesty and awareness, is that it ought not to have known hereditary defects, and the new owner will have the support and guidance of experienced people, and can expect to enjoy a lifetime's fulfilment from the experience of dog ownership. Dogs give us their servitude without question, argument or judgement, and it is our responsibility to respect that generosity in return.

2 BREEDING PRINCIPLES

Each purebred breed of dog was bred by man from particular varieties of dog over a great number of years in order to perform a specific purpose. That is why he has a certain size, shape, conformation and temperament, coupled with balance: this means that he will be sound enough to fulfil his purpose with the required vigour without putting strain on his joints, thereby causing pain or suffering. His purpose should be studied accurately, so that his outline, size and conformation are not distorted through lack of knowledge by an inexperienced or uninformed breeder.

The basic conformation or construction of the dog should be carefully studied and observed before you set about breeding your chosen breed.

THE IMPORTANCE OF CONFORMATION

Conformation, or construction, describes the assembly of the bones (the skeleton), which is a bony framework and consists of bones, ligaments and cartilage. The skeleton protects the organs within the body, and the bones store calcium, phosphorus and other elements, also red blood cells and bone marrow.

Some bones are connected by cartilage-forming levers, which are used in locomotion; they should be positioned to allow the dog easy access of movement with the least effort. Muscle will hold and support the bone correctly and should be well developed; for example, the shoulder is not connected to the frame by bone, only muscle. So the dog should be exercised adequately to keep him fit and in good physical shape.

A Chihuahua has the same number and type of bones as a Great Dane; it is the size and shape that will vary between

This Hungarian Vizsla is of sound construction, giving balance. He is the show champion/Australian champion Hungargunn Bear It'N Mind. (Photo: Lisa Croft-Elliott)

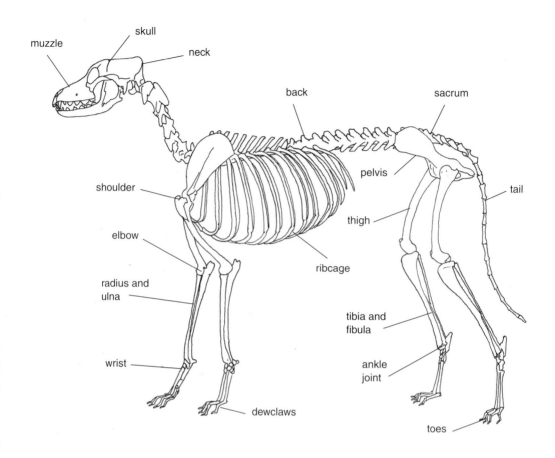

The skeletal structure of the dog.

breeds. Soundness and balance are integral with structure, allowing ease of carriage and freedom in extended movement.

Type is what makes the dog the breed that he is; thus the head shape, expression and ear set are contributors to type. For instance, examples are given of breeds that are quite different in head type and jaw set, yet we should always strive to produce dogs with an adequately proportioned jaw where the teeth are well placed and strong. Breeding any fault knowingly increases the chance of perpetuating the problem. All dogs have forty-two teeth, and full dentition is desirable for the health and well-being of any dog.

A terrier requires a sharp eye and acute hearing, which help him see and hear quick-moving vermin. He also requires big strong teeth contained in a jaw that is powerful for his size, thus enabling him to kill his prey quickly and efficiently, and therefore effectively more humanely, without injury to himself.

A gundog, on the other hand, should display a gentle, kindly temperament. He

ABOVE: The Irish Wolfhound at the top end of the size scale and the Miniature Wirehaired Dachshund at the other end, all champions bred by Zena Thorn-Andrews. (Photo: Eric Smethurst)

RIGHT: The Basenji is alert and lightly-built, with an obliquely set eye and pricked ears.

BELOW: The Hungarian Wirehaired Vizsla has a more rounded skull giving a lower ear set. He has a gentle expression and a big nose with open nostrils to take in scent.

ABOVE: The shape of head and facial expression of the Bulldog are quite different from those of the average dog. However, Bulldogs can still be healthy and fit, as is the case with this dog.

ABOVE: The Parson Russell Terrier has the keen, intelligent expression so typical of a terrier.

BELOW: The shape and the hair growth pattern on the head of the Shih Tzu give a 'chrysanthemum-like' effect.

ABOVE: The Whippet's power, elegance and grace is shown to advantage on the move.

RIGHT: The media often decries the Bulldog, but Paul and Maria Harding's bitch is totally balanced, sound, healthy and clean – a beautiful example of the breed.

also requires a strong jaw and full dentition, enabling him to carry heavy game gently and without inflicting damage, so that his prize is fit for human consumption.

The Whippet is built on sleek, aerodynamic lines, required for fleetness of foot, being a sight hound; he, too, needs a powerful snapping jaw, for the rapid killing of rabbits and rats – yet his muzzle is tapering and clean cut, in harmony with his overall smooth lines.

By contrast, the Bulldog standard requires the flews to be thick and broad so they hang over the lower jaws at the sides, not at the front, but covering all the teeth. The broad, massive jaw is square,

and the lower jaw projects considerably in front of the upper (known as an undershot bite); he was originally bred for bull baiting, and this formation of jaw allowed him to breathe whilst his jaw was locked on to a bull's nose.

The majority of standards ask for a scissor bite, and each breed standard will clearly state whether an undershot or scissor bite is required. No standard asks for a wry mouth or twisted jaw or teeth, which are severe faults, and dogs displaying these should not be bred from.

Fanciers of a variety of different breeds often refer to 'their' breed as a 'head breed'; however, this can lead to the production of puppies that excel in head

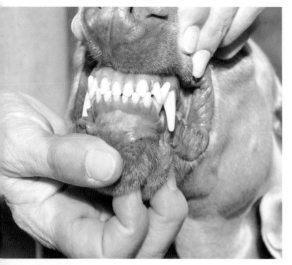

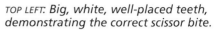

TOP LEFT: *Big, white, well-placed teeth, demonstrating the correct scissor bite.*

BELOW LEFT: *Most breeds ask for a scissor bite or reverse scissor, but a mouth such as this is wrong and if the dog is bred from the fault will be perpetuated.*

BELOW: *The front on the Bull Terrier is typical of the bull breeds, having more width in the chest, coupled with the correct formation of the shoulder to fit neatly around the bigger spring of rib required, yet allowing freedom of movement.*

type at the expense of other points of conformation, so the whole dog should always be considered: type, health and soundness in equal proportions.

Following on from the head, the neck should be long enough to fulfil the dog's needs, with muscle to support the neck vertebrae and give strength. The length of neck will be determined by conformation of the shoulder blade – thus an upright blade gives a shorter neck.

The blade from the withers leads to the point of shoulder, which is connected to the upper arm via a joint that allows the leg to reach forwards. The upper arm must be in harmony with the conformation of the blade to allow the forward reach of the front leg through the shoulder. If the blade is upright and the upper arm short, there is no leverage to allow the foreleg to extend, and this will only allow a short, choppy stride. Otherwise the leg will be thrown out to compensate, and the lack of smooth, effective action will put stress on joints and therefore pressure on the whole body. Consequently, breeds designed to gallop need the placement of the shoulder blade and the length and return of the upper arm to be such that the angle formed is approximately 90 degrees when the dog is standing so that the foreleg is perpendicular to the ground.

Obviously the construction of the front in different breeds will not always be the same. For example, in breeds that have short legs on a strong body with deep ribs, for the shoulder to be laid back and the upper arm to fit round the deep chest with spring of ribs, the forearm has to be curved around the ribs otherwise the front legs would be too wide apart. If the forearms are too curved or weak the front will be crooked. Breeds requiring a barrel chest have shoulder placement that comes straight off the side of the rib, so that effectively the front legs stand wide apart.

The dog has thirteen pairs of ribs, the length and spring of which, whatever their shape, protect the 'engine' of the dog – the heart, lungs and so on.

Many breeds require straight front legs, yet must have some give in the pastern, which is effectively the shock absorber.

Feet will be different from one breed of dog to another, and the length of the toes, the foot size and knuckling will be adapted to the work the dog has been bred for. However, every dog needs good feet to last his whole life, so quality pads are important. In some breeds the feet are allowed to turn out slightly, but too much is a weakness, so moderation should be observed.

The weakest part of the vertebrae is

The more typical 'terrier front', narrower to allow the dog to 'go to ground'.

Straight front legs with no weakness in the pasterns, and elbows neat, not sticking out.

TOP RIGHT: *A Griffon Bruxellois is classed as a toy dog but still needs balance and width of chest to move easily.*

TOP LEFT: *The 'dwarf' front: because the body is deep and the legs short, the upper arm needs to bend slightly round the ribs, to provide neat elbows and freedom of movement. This is shown to advantage by the excellent Cardigan Corgi. (Photo: Lisa Croft-Elliott)*

This beautiful yellow Labrador displays the correct angle of shoulder blade and upper arm, with complementary hind angulation, which will provide true foot fall when moving.

the loin, so quality muscling should support this.

The angle in the hindquarters should reflect the forequarters, otherwise the dog will not move in a balanced way, and this will put pressure on varying parts of the body.

We should be aware of a fault that has been creeping in to some breeds over the last few years: lack of angulation in the forequarters, coupled with an overlong stifle to hock bone. This fault will limit the dog's over-reach – the amount by which his back legs pass his front legs – or will cause him to crab (when the back legs move to the side of the body). The dog will instinctively always try his utmost to maximize his stride, but in this case his frame will probably 'wear out' at a relatively early age, and arthritis or other ailments will develop.

In some gundog circles, a small number in the die-hard shooting fraternity will mock 'show-bred' gundogs as 'just being pretty' but lacking instinct, whilst those few who primarily show their gundogs will decry the working dogs as unsound. Fortunately, most will work together to produce sound dogs that retain their instinct. The health of the dogs is their primary concern, over and above their own ego.

Tail set will vary according to the positioning of the croup. The tail is an important part of the dog, in that it is used to display temperament and mood, and can alert his handler to where he is. In the case of a terrier going to ground and becoming trapped, the owner can grab it to pull him out; and a Labrador will use it as a rudder when retrieving from water.

The dog's coat can play an important part in protecting it from cold, heat or foreign bodies and undergrowth.

It is said that 'a good horse is never a bad colour', and so it may be said of the dog – although because breeds were created by originally crossing types of dog, undesirable aspects sometimes developed, including bad colour. To maintain type it is never of benefit to breed from dogs that do not conform to the required points, and colour is one such aspect – although colour does not carry quite the significance of construction or disposition.

The Importance of the Breed Standard

As well as studying conformation and structure, it is important to study the standard of the desired breed in order to comply with the idiosyncrasies of that breed, therefore remaining sympathetic to the breed type. The breed standard is the blueprint for the breed.

UNDERSTANDING THE KENNEL CLUB BREED GROUPS

So how do you choose which dog is the one for you? Purebred pedigree dogs registered with the kennel club are categorized into seven groups. There are 210 breeds currently registered with the KC. The rest of this chapter gives a very brief description of the main dog breeds.

The Hound Breeds

There are thirty-six hound breeds, and these comprise sight hounds and scent trailing, hunting dogs. The following breeds are sight hounds: the Afghan, the Asawakh, Basenji, Cirneco Dell'Etna, Deerhound, Greyhound, Ibizan, Irish Wolfhound, Pharaoh, Portuguese Podengo, Saluki and Whippet. Even though they are dissimilar in shape, size and coat, all these hounds are highly active, with great speed of movement.

One of the sight hounds, the greyhound has great agility and speed. (Photo: Lisa Croft-Elliott)

Dignified, aloof, alluring – Owen Greechan's multi-titled Rashid Ebn Hugo Von Haussman at Myhalston, displays exquisitely the characteristics of the Afghan Hound.

The French word *bas* means low, and is the origin of the English name 'Basset' Hound, meaning 'low to the ground'. The Basset, Basset Fauve de Bretagne, Basset Bleu de Gascogne, Basset Griffon Vendeen (*grand*), and Basset Griffon Vendeen (*petit*) are all sturdy hunting hounds that are short in the leg (low to the ground). The Hamiltonstovare, Grand Bleu de Gascogne, the Beagle and Foxhound are also pack hounds, as is the bloodhound; the Bloodhound has an amazing ability to follow human scent for excessively long periods over rough terrain. The Borzoi is another hunting dog, originally used by the Russian aristocracy to hunt wolves.

In the UK we recognize six varieties of Dachshund: there are two categories, miniature and standard, and both sizes have smooth-haired, long-haired and wire-haired varieties. They were bred to go down a badger sett and kill the incumbent badger, and although small, they are immensely strong with powerful jaws. There was an account of a family in Florida whose Dachshund was devoured by an alligator; distraught, they returned home – but in the morning the dog was sitting on the doorstep waiting to be let in! They later found a dead alligator with its stomach ripped open!

TOP LEFT: *This Beagle, Ch Dialynne Tolliver of Tragband, bred by Melanie Spavin, is owned and campaigned to record wins by Andrew Brace. Mikey subsequently became an important sire in the breed, producing many champions. (Photo: Sally Anne Thompson)*

TOP RIGHT: *Breeders Gavin and Sara Robertson with their Basset Griffon Vendeens (petit) and Basset Fauve de Bretagne. (Photo: Lisa Croft-Elliott)*

BELOW: *The word elegant springs to mind when one sees the Borzoi.*

ABOVE: Cavill's Finnish Spitz, alert and with a profuse coat to protect against the harsh winters. (Photo: A. and D. Cavill)

BELOW: Middleton's Norwegian Elkhound, champion Ithim Angus Suim.

From Scandinavia comes the Finnish Spitz and Norwegian Elkhound; the former is used to hunt small birds, and gives tongue as it does so, which is very curious. Both breeds have thick coats.

The Otterhound is rugged enough to cover the ground, but his main purpose is to hunt in water. The Segugio Italiano and the Sloughi are both elegant, with a lithe, racy physique; both are keen hunters.

The Gundog Breeds

There are also thirty-six gundog breeds. These sporting dogs are split into sub-groups consisting of setters and pointers: the English Setter, the Gordon Setter, the Irish Setter, Irish Red and White Setter, and the Pointer. The setters originally belonged to the spaniel family, but over a period of four hundred years they evolved from 'setting' spaniels (used for netting partridge) to the four setters we recognize today. In 1805, Sydenham Edwards published a coloured engraving called 'The Setter' in which the three breeds – the English, Gordon and Irish – were clearly identifiable, proving that by this time at least the three types were individually established.

The original difference between the setter and pointer was that setters were kept for ranging the ground and then standing over birds that would be taken in a net, whereas the pointer, working singly or in a pair, located game that would be taken with a gun. Even in the show type of these breeds, their character can be seen to be good-natured and gentle – but they often disappear 'on a mission' when exercised on open ground, ignoring their owner's calls!

Retrievers

In any research on retrievers, one tends to come back to the Newfoundland. There were two types of Newfoundland dog: the greater and the lesser. It is thought that the Labrador descends from the lesser. One theory is that the flat-coated retriever came about after a crossing of the Newfoundland with the setter. The Golden was in the same category as the Flatcoat, originally identified independently by his colour; likewise the Curlycoat was classified by his curly coat. The Chesapeake Bay is of the same descent but is primarily an excellent water dog, used for retrieving from water, due to his thick, oily coat.

The Nova Scotia Duck-tolling Retriever is thought to go back to a 'smallish ginger dog' used for centuries in Europe to net ducks. His ancestors could include the Brittany Setter, the Chesapeake Bay and the Golden Retriever. He was classified as a breed in Nova Scotia.

Spaniels are amongst the oldest breed of gundog. Generally they will flush game from dense undergrowth; consequently all have a long, protective coat, and are lower to the ground than many other gundogs. Many breeds derive from the original spaniel: the Cocker, bustling and busy and able to work deep in the undergrowth; the Clumber, a heavy dog, methodical and silent in his work; the Field spaniel, low and strong, and ideal for the rough shooter; the Sussex, which moves with a distinctive roll and gives tongue when working; and the Irish Water spaniel, the tallest of the spaniel sub-group, which, as its name suggests, will work water. It has Poodle in its background and is a very old breed. However, the English Springer Spaniel is generally accepted as the oldest of the gundogs, used initially for 'springing' through the undergrowth and flushing out game. The Welsh Springer, too, is pure in origin and

TOP: *This home-bred Clumber Spaniel, show champion Vanitonia U Bet I Am, was top dog in breed in 2010.*

BELOW LEFT: *The largest of the spaniel breeds, the Irish Water Spaniel.*

BELOW RIGHT: *Welsh Springer Spaniel.*

one of the oldest breeds of gundog, lively and active in its quest to flush game.

Many of the above breeds have, over many years, been split into 'working type' and 'show type'. A few stalwarts of these breeds still try to combine soundness, looks and ability in one dog, which is a credit both to the enthusiasts, and to the dogs that compete both in the field and in the show ring.

HPR (Hunt, Point, Retrieve) Breeds

This sub-group, as the name suggests, consists of dogs that are capable of all

ABOVE: This show champion Weimaraner retains the working instinct to hunt.

BELOW: A quality Bracco Italiano, bearing the Bonario affix, showing a typical outline of this breed.

Record-winning breeder Sharon Pinkerton, affix Bareve, showing one of her German Wirehaired Pointer bitches.

aspects of gundog work; therefore the breeds within this group must be quick-thinking and active. These breeds are newer to the British Isles, and initially fanciers looked at how many had become divided into work and show types, and then worked hard to retain dogs which looked good but whose working instinct was still prevalent. Therefore most of the HPR breeds are capable of both work and show.

The Bracco Italiano is a strong, powerful hunter with strong scenting ability. A relatively new breed to the UK, he is making his mark both in the field and in the show ring. The Brittany is the smallest in this category, but is perfectly robust and capable of carrying a hare or a pheasant.

The German Short-haired Pointer (GSP) is very much a dual-purpose dog that will work in the field and win in the show ring. As a ground-scenting dog he is quick when quartering, and is liked on driven shoots for his speed. The German Wire-Haired Pointer (GWP) is a little taller and stronger than the Short-haired, his wiry coat making him an ideal candidate for going into rough undergrowth.

The Hungarian Vizsla has a golden russet-coloured coat which gives him an eye-catching appearance. Smaller in build than his counterparts and more sensitive than the Weimaraner, he is lively and demonstrative in affection. The Hungarian Wire-haired Vizsla is bigger than the short-haired variety, is calm in nature, and works well on fur and feather.

Hardy and untiring, the Italian Spinone is very gentle as well as being a useful worker on all sorts of ground; he has a thick skin and wiry coat.

ABOVE: The Italian Spinone has a unique appearance, and is a very easy-to-live-with dog.

BELOW: A group of our own Weimaraners returning from a run.

The large Munsterlander is a multi-purpose worker that works well with the rough shooter. His coat is feathered, and in colour is always a combination of black or blue roan and white, never brown. The German Long-haired Pointer, on the other hand, is always a combination of brown and white, never black. This one is a newer breed to this country, with generally good conformation.

With his silver-grey coat, the Weimaraner earned himself the nickname 'silver ghost': in the canine world he is the equivalent of the Thoroughbred horse, and we could write reams about his virtues – he is our passion!

The remaining gundogs are the Kooikerhondje, the Kortals Griffon, the Lagotto Romagnolo and the Spanish Water Dog. They are not, at present, part of any sub-group, being newly recognized by the Kennel Club.

The Terrier Breeds

There are twenty-six terrier breeds: all are sporting dogs but they are bred to kill rather than retrieve, although some breeds will work alongside the gundog or hound. Generally they are full of character. Big, white, strong teeth are a primary requirement, and the six lower incisors are essential. Both ear and tail use and set are very important in a terrier, as these often symbolize keenness of character, vital for a dog which must keep vermin in check.

The Airedale Terrier is known as the king of terriers, being the tallest and having attributes that epitomize what most terriers are about. This beautiful breed richly deserves the title.

The Australian Terrier comes in black and tan or red, with a coarse, straight topcoat. Rather longer than tall, his attitude might be described as really 'up for anything'.

From the north of England, the Bedlington is unique in shape with his graceful outline, for a terrier, with a soft, lamb-like coat. He was originally bred to catch rabbits.

The Border is a natural dog, with no extremes. He is expected to go to ground after a fox and also to follow his master's hunter, so he needs to be active and brave.

Both the standard Bull Terrier and the miniature have the same standard, even though they differ in size – the miniature is not more than 14in (35cm) at the withers. One of the main criteria of the breed is that he should have the greatest substance in the smallest area, whilst

A fabulous example of the King of Terriers – the Airedale Terrier. (Photo: Lisa Croft-Elliott)

retaining quality. His head is a quite distinctive egg-like shape.

The mischievous Cairn makes an ideal pet. His weather-resistant double coat is easily looked after. He is a game worker, with small, erect ears.

First bred in 1949 from a Scottish Terrier dog out of a Sealyham bitch, the Cesky Terrier was bred to establish a narrower chest and slightly longer legs for endurance and digging. His prey included fox, rabbit, duck and even wild boar. This is a lovely breed which is, rightly in my view, gaining in popularity.

The name 'Dandie Dinmont' was the name of a character in the novel *Guy Mannering* by Sir Walter Scott, who was pictured with a couple of terriers, representing this breed, so this is where the name comes from. It has an appealing head with big, soulful eyes and a silky topknot. It is a really game terrier.

The Smooth Fox Terrier is alert and full of fire, very smart, and might be compared to a short-backed hunter. It is ultimately brave, and will face anything from rats to foxes. The Wire-haired Fox Terrier has similar attributes with the addition of a dense, wiry coat. Both have V-shaped ears tipping forwards.

Heralding from Ireland, the Glen of Imall is a powerful, strong chap, longer in the body than tall, with a medium-length, harsh topcoat with a soft undercoat. Nimbler than he looks, he works quietly.

The Irish Terrier is taller than many terriers and racy, never stocky or cloddy. He is a bit of a daredevil, and will pursue his quarry, or indeed his master, relentlessly. Another Irish breed is the Kerry Blue. As a youngster his coat will be black, but this should change by the time he is out of the junior class. He does not shed hair, he stands up to 19in (48cm),

The lamb-like features of its coat and its distinct outline make the Bedlington a noticeable example of the terrier group.

ABOVE: *With their egg-shaped head and powerful stance, the Bull Terrier and miniature Bull Terrier are lovely breeds to live with.*

BELOW: *The Cesky Terrier does not have challenge certificates in the UK, but nevertheless has a good following.*

and when his silky coat is trimmed he makes a striking picture. He has a confident, determined nature.

The Lakeland Terrier is friendly, cheeky and fearless. He has a coarse, weather-resistant coat, will run all day, and makes a great companion.

The Manchester Terrier is easily identifiable with his black and tan markings and sleek coat. This elegant ratting dog is thought to have whippet in his genes; he is biddable, and gentle with people.

The Norfolk and Norwich Terriers evolve from the same ancestors. Small, they should not be toy-like, as they should have the strength and bravery to face both fox and badger. The main difference between the breeds is in the character of the ear: the Norfolk has a drop ear, lying close to the cheek, and the Norwich has a prick ear (to remember this difference think of Norwich, a city, so it has a cathedral with a spire that stands straight up). These days the difference between the breeds is more noticeable in that the Norwich tends to be shorter in the back than the Norfolk.

From the Highlands comes the Scottish Terrier. Its head, neck and length of back should be of the same proportions; the body should be powerful, the chest deep and the legs short. The feet must be strong and well padded for digging.

Another terrier that is low to the ground is the Sealyham. Welsh in origin, its predominantly white coat is wiry and long, with a weather-resistant undercoat. It is smart, alert and – as all terriers – fearless.

The Skye is an old Scottish breed. This terrier can be distrustful of those not known to it. In conformation it is very long and low-standing, with a long, straight, coarse coat with a veiling of hair over the eyes. It is more often seen with prick ears, however a drop ear is also correct. It tends to be a one-man dog.

The Scottish Terrier exhibits power on short legs.

Judging a class of Soft-coated Wheaten Terriers.

The Soft-coated Wheaten Terrier stands about 19in (48cm) high. It has a soft, silky, wheaten coat which makes it truly eye-catching. It is an extrovert with natural instincts.

The Staffordshire Bull Terrier is very good with people, making it one of the most popular of all the terriers. It possesses indomitable courage, which can work to its disadvantage, as it will sometimes be used as a guard dog by certain unsavoury characters. Breeders need to 'vet' potential owners rigorously.

The Welsh Terrier was bred to hunt the fox and badger, like other terriers of similar shape and design. It is good with children and therefore makes a good pet and family dog.

The West Highland White Terrier (known as the WHWT) is a very popular pet due to its size, white coat and dark eye, and its cheerful personality. It always exudes energy.

THE UTILITY BREEDS

There are twenty-nine breeds in this group, and they do a variety of jobs. A number of dogs in this group belong to the spitz breeds, which are characterized by an overall wolf-like appearance, with the modification of a tail carried tightly erect and curled over the back, with erect ears and a wedge-shaped head.

The Akita is an upstanding dog bred both as a hunter and fighting dog. It can be dominant, but is also very devoted to its owner.

The Chow Chow is a short-backed, plush-coated dog that came from China to Britain in the eighteenth century. It has guarding instincts and can be a one-man dog. It is not really typical of the spitz breeds.

The Japanese Shiba Inu is a small dog, about 14in (35cm) high; it is alert, and is renowned for its 'shiba scream'. It is increasing in popularity as it is very attractive.

The Eurasier is a new breed to the UK. It is calm and confident in temperament, of medium size, and can be a variety of colours, though it should not have white patches on the body or be completely white or liver.

There are two German Spitz: Klein, the smaller, at 9–11½in (23–29cm), and Mittel at 12–15in (30–38cm). Until recently it was a requirement that judges should measure these breeds. These dogs would have been classed as watchdogs.

Developed in the 1920s, the Japanese Spitz is a small dog with a profuse, pure white coat. It is bold and lively.

The Keeshond stands about 18in (45cm) and is typical spitz in outline. It was used as a watchdog and guard by the Dutch bargemen.

The Schipperke is one of the smaller spitz breeds, most often black in colour,

Ken Sinclair Araki and Neil Smith have had phenomenal success with their Tibetan Terriers. Ken has imported many dogs from overseas to keep producing healthy Tibetans; he feels that too much 'in-breeding' can cause problems in the breed. (Photo: Carol Ann Johnson)

This Mexican Hairless is in excellent condition.

although other whole colours are acceptable; again, it was used to guard the barges in Holland and Belgium.

The Boston terrier is a spruce little American chap, although it obviously has some British influence as there is the bull breed in its background. It is compact, with prick ears and a stylish aura.

Synonymous with Great Britain, the Bulldog is dignified, powerful yet good with children. He has a lot of bad press due to his unusual conformation. Intelligent breeders today are producing dogs that are agile and can breathe without problems; all credit to them.

The Canaan Dog is generally accepted as a guarding breed, the national breed of Israel. It is of medium size, with prick ears, alert and active. It has not long been shown in the UK, but is certainly making its mark.

The Dalmatian is distinguishable by his spotted coat, be it black or liver spotted. Known as a carriage dog, he would run along under the carriages during Regency times. He should be well muscled with clean lines.

The French Bulldog has obvious bull breed influence. He has bat ears, which are peculiar to him. He makes a good family dog with his fun-loving nature.

The Lhasa Apso comes from Tibet, so needs to be tough to cope with the climate and terrain. He is a happy little dog with a long, straight topcoat, which is often clipped off when he is kept as a pet.

Another dog from Tibet is the Tibetan Spaniel, a delightful little breed with the most alluring head and eye; he is intelligent, and can be assertive. There is also the Tibetan Terrier, square in outline and with a long, straight coat, much like human hair in texture. He is the tallest of the Tibetan breeds, standing up to 16in (40.5cm).

The Mexican Hairless is registered with the Kennel Club in this group and is on the import register, with an interim standard, with no CCs on offer. The breed was deemed sacred by the Aztecs. It is a very old breed, which was in danger of dying out, but the FCI registered a breeding programme in 1956.

The Schnauzer and the Miniature Schnauzer are the small and medium of the Schnauzer family. There is also a giant variety, in the 'working' group. All are the same basic shape, very clean in outline with a coarse, wiry coat. This can be stripped or clipped (if a pet), leaving the face and leg hair which enhances the appearance. Stocky yet sprightly, the miniature version in particular makes a good family pet.

In the UK there are three sizes of Poodle: standard, miniature and toy. There is a general misconception that Poodles are snappy and stupid; however, nothing could be further from the truth. They are highly intelligent, yet have a blithe, appealing temperament. They come in various solid colours. Their profuse coat does not shed. Originally the 'pompoms' that covered the joints were manicured to protect the joints when the dog retrieved from water.

The Shar Pei is easily recognized for his excessively wrinkly skin. When he was first introduced to this country, many had problems, often genetic, mainly due to skin entropion and sores between the wrinkles. By careful breeding, the breed

LEFT: The Miniature Poodle. (Photo: Lisa Croft-Elliott

BELOW: This picture shows off delightfully the expression of the Shih Tzu.

has benefited considerably and the majority are sound and fit.

The Shih Tzu is Chinese in origin. The head can be likened to a chrysanthemum, due to the way the hair grows, which easily distinguishes him from the Lhasa. Quite the extrovert, he is very friendly, making him a great pet.

THE WORKING BREEDS

There are thirty-six working breeds, The working and pastoral breeds were together in the working group. With the recognition of more breeds the number of breeds became too many to be manageable for one group; consequently we now have seven groups in the UK.

The Alaskan Malamute is the largest and most powerful of the spitz breeds. He is a strong dog, pulling sledges for long periods. As his name suggests, he has a thick coat for warmth. He is a very striking dog.

The Beauceron stands up to 27in (67cm) tall, and is powerful and active. He does not like being left alone. He is one of France's oldest breeds and has worked shepherding around the plains of Paris since the sixteenth century. He is also a good guard dog.

The Bernese Mountain Dog is a beautiful Swiss dog, with his coal-black coat with tan points and white on his head, chest and paws. He is used for herding sheep and cattle, but also as a draft dog. He would pull a cart, has a lovely temperament, and is good with children.

The Bouvier de Flandres is a rugged chap, guarding and herding cattle in France and Belgium. He has strong bone, a short, well-developed body, and an abundant coarse coat.

The Smooth-coated Boxer hails from Germany. He is full of exuberance and tends to jump up, almost 'boxing' in play. Often referred to as a 'head' breed, devotees today concentrate on the whole dog, and as such he is often seen in the placings in the group ring.

The Bullmastiff is a British breed that came about from the pairing of the old English Mastiff and the Bulldog. He is intent on protecting his family, yet is calm and makes a good house dog. Powerful in build, he stands up to 26in (40cm).

The Canadian Eskimo dog is a relatively rare breed. Typically Spitz in shape, he stands no more than 27½in (68cm) and can be a variety of colour combinations, which means that he is not always easily identifiable. He can have any eye colour except blue. He can catch an 18in (45cm) fish and eat it before it hits the ground, such is his dexterity.

The German-born Dobermann is an elegant, clean dog. Predominantly black and tan in colour – though he can be brown, blue or fawn with the typical markings – this smooth-coated breed is often used for police work, due to his tracking ability and intelligence. The German Pinscher is of the same family: between 17–20in (43–50cm) in height, he is quick-witted, vibrant and intelligent. He would hunt vermin.

With his thick, loose skin and powerful build, the Dogue de Bordeaux sets an imposing figure. He is vigilant and makes a good guard dog, but is gentle and very affectionate. He needs a committed breeder.

The Giant Schnauzer is the largest of this family. Strong, with a striking outline, he is capable of speed and endurance. His coarse coat is weather-resistant. He is in the working group, as opposed to the utility group with his cousins, due to his size and his ability to herd and guard.

The Siberian Husky is slightly built and has a strong following, both working (above – photo Chris Kisko) and showing (below – photo Jon Kendrew).

ABOVE: A Dobermann puppy starting out on his show career.

BELOW: This young Giant Schnauzer cuts a typical, quality outline.

Despite their size and powerful appearance, Mastiff breeds are generally gentle dogs. (Photo: Lisa Croft-Elliott)

Generally a gentle giant, the male Great Dane stands up to 30in (75cm), and the bitch 28in (70cm). He is well boned and sleek, with a dignified air about him. The negative is that, due to his size, he can be a short-lived dog. However, we have had a Great Dane swimming in our hydrotherapy pool that lived until he was twelve years old.

The Greenland Dog is new to this country but is thought to descend directly from wolves. A member of the spitz breeds, he is a sled and guard dog.

The Hovawart is a medium-sized dog with a medium-long, dense coat that comes in black, blonde or black and gold. He is a working and companion dog, used in the Black Forest region of Germany; his history goes back to many regions in the Mediterranean countries.

The Leonberger is a German breed, produced by crossing the St Bernard and the Newfoundland, so it is not surprising that he stands up to 32in (80cm) and is powerfully made. He is sensible in nature and makes a good guarding dog. He has a medium long coat with an undercoat.

The Mastiff is a very old British breed. It is fortunate that he is calm in nature, as he is truly massive. He should also present a quality, balanced picture throughout.

The massive frame of the Neapolitan Mastiff is typified by the loose-fitting skin; the pendulous dewlap gives the impression that the head is even bigger than it is. However, the skin should not be so loose as to cause health problems or lack of quality.

So many breeds owe their evolution to the Newfoundland, that gentle giant. He is featured in the book Peter Pan, as 'nanny' to the children. This beautiful, big, well-coated dog is known for his swimming abilities. To this day he is quite capable of rescuing someone in distress from the water, even from a row-boat.

The Portuguese Water Dog is called the 'fisherman's dog'. He is recognizable by his profuse wavy coat to the front of his body, and the close coat from beyond his ribs.

In intelligent hands, the Rottweiler is a true gentleman.

Tan Negrecha's Chandlimore St Bernards are clean, sound and powerful.

The coal-black coat with rich tan points on a strong body instantly identifies the Rottweiler. He is a natural guarding German breed. In intelligent hands he is a gentleman. Years ago he was acquired by people wanting a 'macho' dog and gained a bad press, but fortunately this reputation is changing.

The imposing stature of the Russian Black Terrier with his double wavy coat and the furnishings on his head is enough to ward off intruders. A guard dog, he is nevertheless confident and even-tempered.

Known as the 'Swiss rescue dog' with brandy strapped to his collar, the St Bernard is one of the largest, in every way, of all breeds of dog. Stable and dependable, it is important that all points of this breed are balanced and full of quality.

The Siberian Husky, another member of the Spitz breeds, is a medium-sized sled dog. He should not carry his tail tightly over his back, as do many spitz. He can have eyes that are half blue /half brown, (known as parti-coloured) or one blue and the other brown.

The Tibetan Mastiff was found in the foothills of the Himalayas on the border with Tibet. He is a strong dog with a quality coat to protect against the inclement weather he would face, with a bushy tail. He is used as a guard dog.

THE PASTORAL BREEDS

There are thirty-three pastoral breeds.

At up to 32in (80cm) tall and powerfully built, the Anatolian Shepherd is an imposing dog that would guard flocks of sheep. Although he can be very much the gentle giant, he is not for the faint of heart.

The Australian Cattle Dog is highly thought of in his country of origin. He is not only capable of moving cattle, he will single-mindedly guard both them, his ranch and his master.

The very appealing Australian Shepherd, a herding breed, has quickly become increasingly popular, particularly as a show dog. He is intelligent and of even temperament, with a thick, weather-resistant coat.

At a maximum of 22in tall and of lean build, the Bearded Collie is lively and active. His long, coarse coat should be free from curl and left untrimmed.

There are four varieties of Belgian Shepherd Dog: the Groendael is black, with limited white and frosting. He has an abundant outer coat that is quite harsh in texture, fringing on the legs and tail, and, particularly in dogs, more hair and quite a ruff around his neck. This is the same for the Tervueren's coat, although his colour can be any shade of red, fawn and grey with black overlay. The Lackenois has a coat that is harsh and wiry with no curl, and the tail should not have feather. He is reddish fawn and has black shading mainly on the face. The Malinois's hair is short, predominantly on the head and lower legs, but he has a woolly undercoat and quite a bushy tail. He has the same colouring as the Tervueren. All have the same standard, and are strongly built yet graceful. They are used to guard, and as sheepdogs.

The Bergamasco is a medium-sized sheepdog. He is grey in colour, either solid or patched with black, and heavily coated; some white is allowed, as is 'isabella' (fawn).

The Border Collie is probably the most popular of the sheepdogs. He moves with his head down. He is alert and responsive, which makes him a well-liked choice for obedience work.

From Brie in France, the Briard is a medium to large dog with a beautiful flowing coat and dense undercoat. He is very supple and active. Quite the extrovert, his duties would include guarding the flock as well as herding.

The Rough and Smooth Collies are basically the same breed, apart from coat, which is depicted in the names. The *Lassie* films of the 1940s gave fame to the Rough-coated Collie and possibly helped to make him so popular. He is eye-catching with his beautiful full coat. The Smooth-coated Collie has much the same features but the smooth coat shows off his outline more clearly. Both are loyal and dignified in character.

The German Shepherd Dog (GSD) is still referred to as the 'Alsatian' in some quarters. His standard can read differently or be interpreted as such by many. Controversy abounds as to this breed's soundness; however, I have often judged excellent specimens. He was originally bred as a sheep-herding dog and guard of his flock. Such is his intelligence and versatility that police and the military use him, and he is much sought after for obedience and working tests. To see a GSD gaiting is a breathtaking sight.

The Estrela Mountain Dog's height can be up to 28½in (72cm) and he is described as well built, so this dog has a commanding presence. Nevertheless he also has the advantage of having an exemplary temperament, despite being bred as a guard dog.

The Hungarian Puli is identifiable by his corded coat. Standing up to 17½in (45cm) tall, he is a sheep-herder; Hungarian in ancestry and square in outline, he carries his head and tail high, and rather resembles 'a push-me pull-you'.

Another Hungarian corded breed is the Komondor. He is altogether bigger, being up to 31½in (79cm) tall. He is always white in colour. Before his coat cords as an adult, he can almost take on the appearance of a young Old English Sheepdog.

The Lancashire Heeler is a charming breed. This short-legged, black-and-tan herding breed is gutsy and full of northern character. It is thought there is Manchester Terrier influence, and he is 'wick' enough for ratting.

The Maremma Sheepdog is large, big-coated and white in colour. He guards flocks and property in Italy to this day. He is lively and intelligent.

The German Shepherd Dog has had an unfair pummelling from various quarters for a while, the theory being that the breed is exaggerated and not sound. Here is an example of a beautifully constructed dog. No dog that moves this well could do so if he had weakness in any area of assembly. (Photo: Lisa Croft-Elliott)

ABOVE LEFT: The Hungarian Puli has a corded coat and his tail is virtually the same height as his head. (Photo: Lisa Croft-Elliott)

ABOVE RIGHT: The distinct, heavily corded coat of the Komondor does not impede movement, as can be easily seen here. (Photo: Lisa Croft-Elliott)

Very typically spitz in outline, the Norwegian Buhund is a smart, medium-sized, energetic dog.

The Old English Sheepdog's popularity grew when he was used in advertisements for paint. He is a strong, square dog with a profuse, shaggy coat. He is grey, blue or grizzle on his body, with a white head, neck, forequarter and tummy. This makes him desirable, but the coat requires time and work.

Often born without a tail, the Polish Lowland Sheepdog is similar in style and shape to the Bearded Collie, but slightly smaller.

On a larger scale is the Pyrenean Mountain Dog. He is strongly made and not built for speed, yet he has a certain elegance. Mainly white, he would protect the flock from wolves. His standard demands that he has double dew claws on his hind legs.

The Pyrenean Sheepdog is medium to small, very alert and active, with quite a long, coarse coat. He has rather flat, lean feet, which act as snowshoes.

The Samoyed is a striking, primarily white, spitz breed; he has dark pigmentation, which enhances his laughing expression. His nature also reflects this.

He, too, has rather flat, lean feet, which act as snowshoes.

The Shetland Sheepdog is a good-natured, small dog, and therefore very popular both as a family pet and show dog. He is very glamorous with his thick, profuse coat.

The Swedish Lapphund is an elegant, medium-sized spitz, used to herd sheep and reindeer. The Swedish Vallhund is a small but powerful spitz; an old breed, it is said to have been known to the Vikings.

Both the Cardigan and Pembroke Welsh Corgis stem from the same basic stock, and only split into two breeds in the 1930s. They have distinct differences: the Cardigan has somewhat larger ears set a little wider apart than the Pembroke's; he has round, tight feet, and is rather longer in the body than the Pembroke. He also has a longer tail. He is not as popular as the Pembroke. The Pembroke is only allowed self colours of red, sable, fawn and black and tan, with or without white on the legs, brisket, neck and head. Both are low to the ground, brave and active.

THE TOY BREEDS

There are twelve toy breeds. Toy dogs were initially developed to ease the lifestyle and provide pleasure for the wealthy – and even today there are

The Shetland Sheepdog is popular both as a family pet and as a show dog. (Photo: Lisa Croft-Elliott)

The Pembroke Welsh Corgi is the more popular of the two varieties of Corgi. (Photo: Lisa Croft-Elliott)

'celebrities' who have a 'toy' as a status symbol and carry the dog around in the designer handbag: some things never change!

Many of these breeds don't have a height standard, but are measured by weight.

The Affenpinscher has a monkey-like expression and the mischievousness to match. He has a rough, coarse coat that requires no trimming. He has records dating back to the seventeenth century in Europe.

The Australian Silky Terrier descends from the Australian and Yorkshire Terriers. Not surprisingly he is quick-witted and has terrier tendencies. He has a long, straight, silky coat.

The Bichon Frise is a pure white, glamorous breed with dark pigment. His coat is hypoallergenic. He is very active: one of the best moving dogs I have judged was a Bichon. His name in French means 'curly lap dog'. The aristocracy in Europe fancied this breed.

In the same family is the Bolognese. Quite a rare breed, he is Italian and has had famous admirers, including Madame Pompadour.

Another of this family is the Coton de Tulear. This small white dog is slightly longer than he is tall, with a single coat that is wavy and about 3in (8cm) long, and the texture of cotton.

The Havanese is also included in this family: a small, sturdy dog that can be any colour or combination with a plumed tail set high and carried over his back.

The Maltese is a relation. This proud little dog with his long, straight, silky white coat is eye-catching in the group ring. The coat does need careful attention.

ABOVE: *The Cavalier King Charles Spaniel has a sweet nature and is deserving of being one of the most popular pet dogs.*

BELOW: *These two fantastic Chinese Crested dogs are both top winners. The 'hairless' is Lee Cox and Tom Isherwood's Ch. Vanitonia Unwrapped, and the 'powder puff' is Lisa Croft-Elliott and Ms L. Dorris's Am Ch. Chmiel Argoel New Germanika. (Photo: Lisa Croft-Elliott)*

One of the most popular of all dogs is the Cavalier King Charles Spaniel. This breed and the King Charles Spaniel are known to go back centuries. They split into separate breeds in the 1930s. The Cavalier is charming, not yappy, easy to get on with and very pretty: no surprise that people find him so attractive. The King Charles is slightly smaller with a more snub nose and domed head.

The Chihuahua is named after a state and town in Mexico. He may be small, but he thinks he is the biggest dog around! With his big flaring ears and large, round, dark eyes he always 'struts his stuff'! He comes in two varieties, the smooth- or long-coated. He is much favoured by those who want a dog in their handbag!

The Chinese Crested also comes in two varieties, the hairless and the powder puff. The hairless has a fine, smooth skin, which is warm to the touch; he has soft, fine hair pluming his scalp, lower legs and tail. The powder puff is veiled, with a long, soft coat all over his body. The breed is racy and fine boned.

The English Toy Terrier is a smooth-coated, clearly marked, black-and-tan dog with a set pattern for his markings. He has candle flame-shaped ears, which are distinctive of the breed. He is alert, much like a terrier.

This Griffon Bruxellois has the breed's typical monkey-like face.

Another with a monkey face is the Griffon Bruxellois. This bright, rough-coated chap has small, semi-erect ears and dark, round eyes which give him an alert expression. He is lively, with terrier tendencies.

The Italian Greyhound can appear aloof, but is gentle and brave. He is in fact the Greyhound in miniature, and is loving and a wonderful companion.

Described as an oriental aristocrat, the Japanese Chin has a large head in proportion to his body, with a short muzzle. He has large eyes, and it is a feature of the breed that he shows the white of his eye in the inner corner, giving him a look of astonishment. His plush, straight, silky coat makes him a striking picture.

The Lowchen is referred to as the 'little loin dog', because he is trimmed to leave hair on his forequarters and clipped short on his hindquarters, leaving a plume on the end of the tail. He is measured by height, and at a maximum of 13in (33cm) is the tallest in this group.

The Miniature Pinscher, commonly referred to as the 'Min Pin', is the smallest of the Pinschers, but typical in colour coat and style. He is fearless, and moves with a typical hackney action.

Bright and dainty, the charming Papillon is known as such due to his very large, mobile ears, rounded at the tips, which give him the look of a butterfly. His coat is long and full, without undercoat, adding to his charm.

The Pekingese ancestry can be traced back to the Tang dynasty. His short-legged body is topped by a proportionately large head, a feature of the breed that needs to be studied as a priority. His coat is profuse, with a mane that forms a cape round his short neck. He has a thick undercoat, so meticulous grooming is necessary.

The Pomeranian is the smallest of the spitz. With his soft, fluffy undercoat, topped by a long, straight, coarse topcoat, he looks rather like a puffball. He is a vivacious little dog, always on the go.

The Pug is a rugged character and always up for a game. He constantly makes you smile with his mischievous, expressive, large dark eyes. He makes a marvellous pet and companion.

The Yorkshire Terrier is in the terrier group in some counties. In full coat he is a joy to look at, but that fine silky coat needs a great deal of care and attention. A brave little dog, nothing fazes him.

Not all these breeds are qualified for Challenge Certificate status. A new breed will first go on to the import register until the KC deems that it is eligible for transfer on to the breed register. So when you choose a dog for breeding, it should be for what he is, and not just because of his aesthetic appeal.

3 BASIC GENETICS

Genetics is the study of heredity and variation in organisms, and being a science, fills most people with fear and dread! However, on closer inspection it is something that is universally recognized and observed by dog breeders and farmers – in fact all good stockmen/women – by instinct. Probably farmers and horticulturists follow the science of genetics more than dog breeders, because they breed for production attributes and are not influenced by the general public. Selection can be made scientifically, in that, for example, a particular bull which is proven to carry the gene for production of a high percentage of butterfat in the milk, will be selected to be used on cows from a dairy herd. His female progeny will most likely have inherited the gene, making their milk production more cost-effective.

Similarly, certain breeds of cattle have been bred to develop exaggerated muscle on the more expensive cuts of meat, giving a better killing out percentage, and therefore more profit.

WHAT ARE GENES?

Traits are passed on through breeding, via genetics; for example, a child brought up without one parent present will grow

These Pointer puppies show that, even though different in colour, family looks are evident. (Photo: Jason Lynn)

up with some characteristics that the absent parent shows themselves, even though the child is unaware of these hereditary idiosyncrasies. In the same way, genetic problems could be inherited from the parents.

All dogs evolve from wolves, so all dogs have the same genetic information inborn from the universal ancestor. At present there are about 400 breeds registered by the various kennel clubs around the world.

The canine genome consists of 40,000 diverse genes and contains all the genetic information necessary to specify a dog. Genes are made of a chemical called deoxyribonucleic acid, commonly known as DNA, and the plan that a gene holds is carried in the chemical structure of the DNA molecule that makes a particular gene.

The DNA molecule is shaped rather like a corkscrew ladder; the 'rungs' are four different types. The information in DNA comes in the way those types are ordered along the molecule, rather like dots and dashes in Morse code, so can be 'read' to obtain data.

Genes are particular sections of the DNA molecule, and it is the genes that are 'read' to make proteins. These are used as building blocks; the proteins build individually or in groups and determine the characteristics of the final dog.

Genes are grouped in special structures called chromosomes (which are essentially DNA molecules). Each chromosome contains tightly packed molecules of DNA, and these 'transport' the genes from generation to generation.

The name 'locus' is given to the place that the gene occupies in the chromosome; genes occupying the same locus are called 'alleles' or 'allelomorphs'. Animals with matching alleles are referred to as 'homozygous' for that particular gene; those with different alleles are known as 'heterozygous'. The dog has thirty-nine pairs of chromosomes. Each parent contributes one copy of each chromosome via the sperm or the egg.

The process of producing sperm and eggs is obviously crucial in the inheritance of genes; this is called meiosis. During this process a special diploid 'stem' cell, with two copies of each chromosome, divides into sperm or egg cells. These are known as haploid 'gamete' cells and contain just a single set of chromosomes. The copy of each chromosome that a sperm and an egg receive when the diploid cell divides is determined randomly; consequently each sperm and egg is different.

Naturally, when a sperm fertilizes an egg, the chromosomes from the sperm combine with those from the egg, resulting in a diploid cell with two copies of each chromosome – maternal and paternal. This diploid cell, called a 'zygote', is the starting point of the embryo and ultimately gives rise to all the cells of the resulting dog.

Sex-linked Inheritance

Every mammal has various paired chromosomes that are similar in look, and line up with each other during zygote production. The chromosomes that determine the sex of an animal are called X and Y. Normal division of chromosomes during meiosis will put one or the other in each sperm or ovum. Females are always X X, therefore ova are always X. Males are X Y, therefore sperm can be X or Y; therefore the sire determines the sex of the offspring.

The Y chromosome only carries the fact that a male animal is male. Any genes associated with the X chromosome are known as 'sex-linked' genes. Females can be homozygous or heterozygous sex-linked genes. Males can only be hemizygous, having only a single copy of the X-linked gene. This also means that any defects on the X chromosome that a male receives will be apparent in the animal, as there is no alternative to be expressed. For example, if a female who is a carrier for a harmful recessive gene (Xx) passes that harmful gene to the daughter, the daughter will be an unaffected carrier. However, the son will be affected if he receives that gene. Haemophilia is an example, though this is rare in dogs.

DOMINANT/RECESSIVE GENES

Inheritance from parent to offspring is the most basic form of gene transmission.

Established earlier, every dog has two copies of each – one from the sire and one from the dam – and the combination of alleles it has is known as the 'genotype'. Autosomal genes are those that are not on the sex chromosome. How genes interact with each other, with other genes and with the environment will determine what traits you will see expressed in the dog, referred to as 'phenotype'.

The basic mode of inheritance is dominance. From a pair of genes inherited, either one, or both, may be dominant or recessive. A dominant gene will always overrule a recessive one, but if two copies of the recessive gene are present then the recessive genotype will be expressed. Take, for example, the colours black and chocolate in labradors. The allele for black is dominant (B); the allele for chocolate is recessive (b). One copy of the dominant black allele (Bb) produces black; also two copies of the black allele will produce black (BB). To be chocolate, however, because chocolate is the recessive allele, it must have two copies (bb).

If a black labrador carries the recessive allele chocolate, then it could produce chocolate offspring as long as another

The chocolate Labrador.

recessive chocolate allele is passed on from the mate. A chocolate-to-chocolate pairing will only produce chocolate, as both parents must be homozygous recessive (bb). In order to create black the chocolate must be bred to black. Chocolate colour, being recessive, can skip generations of puppies, with the gene still being passed on but masked by the dominant black gene (for example Bb). The chocolate phenotype may then reappear again several generations later.

Simply looking at a dog cannot determine what genes a said dog carries.

However, knowing the phenotypes of dogs within the pedigree, you can work out which dogs in the pedigree may carry the recessive gene: thus if a black dog has a chocolate parent, the black dog will be heterozygous (Bb), and if the heterozygous dog is then mated to a dog with at least one copy of chocolate allele, this gives that dog at least a 50/50 chance of producing puppies with chocolate allele.

The reason we had an English Setter was because my sister had an orange belton English Setter and decided to have puppies. The bitch was duly mated to an orange belton sire, and we booked to have a blue belton bitch – all parties being naive in dog breeding. Following on from the observations concerning black and chocolate Labradors, all the resulting puppies were, of course – orange belton (since both parents were orange belton, even though orange is recessive).

Heredity means the genetic transmission of physical or mental characteristics from one generation to another – from parents to offspring. The benefits of this in dogs is that a family or handler wanting a particular breed, or the look of the variety of dog, can research the mannerisms and inherent behavioural character applicable for the intended requirements of the breed, before acquiring a dog, making sure that this type of dog will fit into their lifestyle or requirements. They can also research inherent traits or defects, and can check with the Kennel Club and/or breed societies as to whether

Only orange mated to orange can produce orange in the English Setter.

THE DOMINANT RULES OF INHERITANCE

- The gene or characteristic will always show itself and does not skip generations.
- Only one parent with the dominant gene can affect the offspring to show the same.
- Only dominant genes carry those for dominant characteristics.
- Dominant genes can mask recessive genes.

THE RECESSIVE RULES OF INHERITANCE

- The gene or characteristic can hide and miss one or more generation without being obvious.
- Offspring that inherit identical recessive genes (one from each parent) will illustrate that characteristic, but the parents need not display it.
- Dominant characteristics cannot be masked by recessive genes.
- Any recessive characteristics have to come from both sire and dam.

Simply remember: dominant to dominant can produce recessive, but recessive to recessive can only produce recessive. *So this is how different breeds develop and have qualities that are peculiar to that specific breed.*

the breeder of a litter, from whom the new owner is potentially to acquire a puppy of this breed, has completed health screening.

THE INBREEDING CONTROVERSY

The cataloguing of dogs used for breeding, with their inherent make-up and requirements of function in relation to size and shape, together with temperament, construction and soundness, forms the foundation of a 'pedigree' or purebred dog; thus data can be sourced, collated and stored for future reference. With regard to dog breeding, the public considers this rather more cautiously, probably because a dog is looked upon as part of the family, and therefore human persona are put into the thoughts as to how their pet came into being, without accepting that a dog is an animal and should be bred and treated as such.

Thus at the beginning of this century, all sorts of controversy broke out when various dog-related organizations and television programmes decided to 'expose' breeders of purebred dogs as discreditable because they produced dogs from close matings. They implied that the mating between father /daughter, or son /mother was not only incestuous but actually 'created' genetic defects. Consequently a furore ensued amongst the general public – even though they were, in effect, only supplied with a totally biased opinion.

If one is to produce dogs from a very close mating, as described above, it should only be done with a full quantity of knowledge of the breed and the genetic problems that are evident within the breed. Advice should be sought from a geneticist, since for the future of one's breeding plan and the breed in general this is not a breeding programme to be undertaken lightly or on a whim.

As a result, the Kennel Club had to rethink their views on breeders who practised close breeding. They also had to be seen to do the 'right and moralistic thing' in view of the public, so as not to alienate the masses (whom they naturally preferred to have 'on side' in order to make sure that dogs were bred correctly); therefore in 2008 they amended their code of conduct, banning the registration of progeny produced between close matings. Their code identifies such progeny as follows:

> The offspring are the result of any mating between father and daughter, mother and son or brother and sister, save in exceptional circumstances or for scientifically proven welfare reasons.

However, many of the most prolific champion-producing kennels started their line by producing stock from such close matings, because this had the effect of cementing the desired features, from which they could then build. Intelligent breeders do not interbreed constantly, but use this form of breeding when it is needed to consolidate pertinent points, or to avoid hereditary problems. Obviously not all breeders, however passionate about their breed, have an in-depth knowledge of stock breeding, therefore the inbreeding of very close relatives could result in condensing some genetic problems – another reason for the Kennel Club to introduce this clause.

Consequently the myth persists – usually perpetrated by uninformed media sensationalists – that interbreeding is the cause of genetic problems. But how can that be?

Interbreeding cannot manufacture defects – they are already there (or not), but close breeding has the amplified effect of bringing hidden problems to the fore. Therefore gifted breeders performing their task with an honest approach can select the dogs for breeding that do *not* perpetuate genetic defects – and so in this instance inbreeding can positively enhance the breeding of sound, healthy dogs.

On the other hand, by outcrossing continuously, not only may faults that are hidden appear later, but also the gene pool is so huge that one can never be sure of which genes will marry up, bringing to the forefront temperament, structure and health dispositions, which could make it impossible to pinpoint and avoid problems because of the vastness of the gene pool. Therefore by extensively outcrossing, the origin of genetic problems will become impossible to identify. As a consequence the breeder is unable to eradicate genetic issues by avoiding breeding from carriers.

As a consequence, crossbreeds and mixed breeds are more at risk of having hidden genetic issues due to their immense gene pool. Furthermore when these issues do surface, they are not recorded, but are lost with the demise of the animal concerned. In purebred breeds, data is collated for reference, but this task is impossible in crossbreeds, as no one has any knowledge of the dogs' ancestry.

This contradicts the proposition – and the myth – that crossbreeds are healthier than breeds that have a documented history, and supports the reason to breed pedigree dogs, but with knowledge.

This is harder for newer breeders to do today, as they don't have the big kennels of yesteryear, headed by experienced breeders of long standing who learned the trade through being able to draw on many more dogs from within their lines, and in view of the fact that they had the space and staff to enable them to keep a lot of dogs at their establishment. More practice, more knowledge.

THE THREE METHODS OF BREEDING

So how do you form a line? By honest,

unbiased research: these are the key words in your initial beginnings to breeding dogs:

- Honest: This should be mainly to yourself: can you justify your reasons for breeding, and look at the stock used for breeding objectively?
- Unbiased: Have you the knowledge and strength of your convictions to use the right dog, even if that dog belongs to someone you don't like?
- Research: Study pedigrees, talk to experienced people, and look at stock produced, first hand, so you can see the attributes produced by different kennels within the breed.

Each time you breed, your ethos should be to improve. This will not always happen (nature may produce anomalies), but the aim should be there – why breed not to progress? Therefore start with the best. Foundation stock should be well constructed, balanced, each part working in harmony with the next. The dog should be typical, a good representative of his breed, and have a confident, solid temperament.

Having established that your own dog fulfils all these requirements, you would look for a mate with similar attributes. Remember, to condense the positives one would go back to similar ancestors – hence line breeding

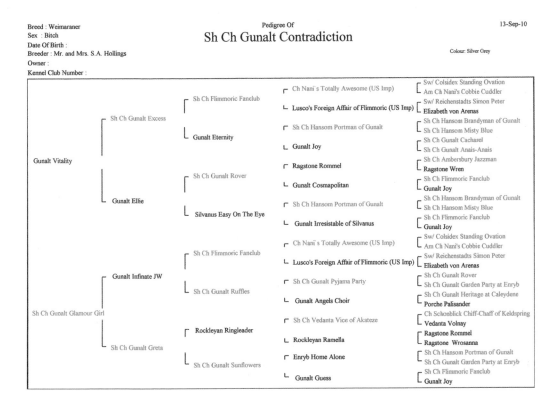

The pedigree of show champion Gunalt Contradiction.

Faults within the breed that are evident in your foundation stock will always be there, and will be capable of appearing when you least expect them. Our original English setter was a little plain in the head and had a low tail-set – twenty years later we were still sometimes seeing these minor faults.

We once considered using a stud dog that had a large amount of our breeding in his pedigree. He was sound, masculine and full of type; he also had the advantage of an impeccable temperament. Upon perusing his pedigree we found a great grand-dam that we knew at first hand had a less than perfect disposition. We really felt that having built our line on soundness, type and temperament it would be a big mistake to introduce such a major fault into our breeding programme, as it would always be there waiting to come out.

If you are serious about the wellbeing of your breed, only consider starting with the best you can and continuing with honesty.

There are three methods of breeding – inbreeding, line breeding and outcrossing:

- Inbreeding: The breeding of close relatives, not separated by more than one generation: father–daughter, mother–son and siblings.
- Line breeding: The mating of dogs with common ancestors: granddaughter–grandsire and uncle–niece: breeding within the lines of a certain strain.

Receiving an award means the judge is of the opinion that the winner is of quality to be reproduced.

Principally, the only difference is the degree of close breeding of relatives. As stated in an earlier chapter, the inbreeding of close relatives has been a major factor in stock breeding for a hundred years and more.

- Outcrossing. The mating of animals within the same breed that are not related closely or related at all (if that is possible).

Outcrossing

It is sometimes said that an outcross will have hybrid vigour. Hybrid means the crossing of two different species, not two different breeds of the same variety, so this in itself is a misnomer. Vigour means 'exuberant' and 'resilient strength of body or mind'. In the author's opinion outcrossing does strengthen the off-spring if the breed has been too closely inbred over a long period: it is nature's way of stopping the 'inbreeding depression', which if lack of fertility and weakness were not to occur, could start to result in progeny being born with severe inherent defects. This is the case both when human intervention occurs but also in the natural state of breeding. Outcrossing does not remove the chance of genetic diseases, it just reduces the number of affected progeny.

Purify by Inbreeding

Every living being has multiple genes in its make-up, but we should presume that every genetic fault in the dog is due to a recessive gene – this may not be the case, but by making this assumption, no faults will be overlooked. So we should not breed from dogs with the same faults in both sire and dam, and should study grandparents and dogs further back within the pedigree. As lay people, this is why it is important to know the animals within the pedigree of a dog we consider using. We can therefore avoid doubling up on genes that may produce faults in health, construction and temperament.

The aim of the dedicated breeder will be to purify his stock, and the surest way to purify a family is by inbreeding, using only the soundest and best stock possible. When and if problems arise, that stock, and subsequent stock from that branch, should be discarded from any further breeding programme.

Over a period of time, wisely used inbreeding can strengthen a strain. However, it must be remembered that whilst line breeding can condense positives, inbreeding plays no favourites, and it will intensify faults as well as virtues. So it is important to learn when it is necessary to introduce a partial outcross to avoid intensifying any recessive factors, or indeed stagnating.

To line breed responsibly we should breed the dog that can breathe with ease, move fluidly, hear and see efficiently, and can fulfil the responsibilities for which he was bred, all without undue effort, therefore giving him a long and stress-free life.

For some reason, any negatives produced in a puppy/puppies are often blamed on the sire. It is also the sire that takes the blame for the number of puppies produced, when it is the dam that produces the eggs! Only if there were a problem with the quality or strength of the sperm would the sire affect the size of the litter, or if the bitch were mated too early or too late, which would reduce the quality of the eggs.

According to geneticists, line breeding can be carried on for many generations without deleterious effects on a breed, as long as the dogs involved have very few hidden genetic disorders.

Screening

Screening is the most effective way to avoid using a dog carrying a known genetic disease. The Kennel Club is furnishing breeders with the chance to screen breeds that are known to carry hereditary defects within that breed; thus it can be established which animals to avoid breeding from, advice that all serious breeders welcome.

So before deciding on which breed of dog to breed from, consult the KC website to find out whether there are hereditary genetic diseases prevalent in your chosen breed. And if there are, make a note of which dogs/lines to avoid before embarking on your breeding programme.

EDUCATION AND THE KENNEL CLUB

It is often said that breeds have changed over the years, usually for the worse. Certainly some breeds have not progressed, though this is primarily through breeder ignorance, and not by intention. In striving to perfect one aspect of the breed they have lost others, often pertaining to health and welfare. However, this tendency is generally in the past, and through edification most have improved.

Breeders are aware that the breed they love should be bred to provide the animals with a long, vigorous, hassle-free life. This has been primarily through education, and the Kennel Club is, and has been, tireless in its approach and support of breeders and the welfare of their charges. They encourage breed clubs to put on seminars, teaching the inexperienced about conformation, health and breed idiosyncrasies. In fact the Kennel Club has purchased a new premises that can accommodate many KC dog-related events, involving interaction with breed clubs, seminars and suchlike. Furthermore through their press office, the KC promotes good dog breeding and owning. Their website encourages potential owners to research breeds to help them decide which breed is suitable for them, and when they have, how to go about finding a reputable and loyal breeder.

The Kennel Club Studbook

Since 1873 the Kennel Club has published a studbook. This revered publication is 'the bible' for the breeder and fancier of dogs. It is produced yearly, and it lists all championship shows from the preceding year, and all the dogs and bitches that qualify for insertion from the previous year.

To qualify for the studbook, a dog must win either a challenge certificate, a reserve challenge certificate (this is best of sex, or reserve best of sex, where challenge certificates are on offer for the breed at a championship show), or a first, second or third prize in the limit or open class at championship shows, depending which band is applicable to that breed.

The bands are laid out by the KC, depending on the breed registrations of the preceding year. There are five bands: A, B, C, D, E. Dogs in band E have the highest registrations and therefore a greater spread of qualifying, whereas breeds in band A have the lowest registrations.

Entry into the studbook can also be gained through winning enough points for a junior warrant (points are accrued from a first place win at open and championship shows, by a dog/bitch under eighteen months of age). Once a dog gains a studbook number, it is his/hers forever.

This is a group of well-bred Golden Retrievers, owned by Lynn Kipps, posed outside their ancestral home, Guisachan in Scotland, showing how biddable and eager to please this breed is. (Photo: Lynn Kipps)

When looking for a dog to use at stud, many will consult the studbook to ascertain his worthiness. If listed, it means that dog has achieved an award giving him merit for inclusion. This confirms that judges have a great responsibility only to award prizes to dogs of worth.

HOW LINES DEVELOP

Breeders often talk about 'their line' when they have bred that particular line for only two or three generations. This does not in fact constitute a line, because in only three generations you are still working on forming a recognizable stamp of the family type of dog that you are aiming for. At least five generations

are needed before you can accept that you have a strain peculiar to your line.

When we started to breed Weimaraners in 1976 our first bitch Amy was a very sound, 'honest' bitch. We looked at the dogs in the breed that were being shown in the ring, and concluded that we most admired the dogs from a particular strain bearing the affix 'Hansom'. We therefore approached the breeder, Mr Dick Finch, and subsequently acquired a male puppy called Sam. This puppy was out of a Hansom bitch by an imported American dog. Sam was mated to Amy, which produced Annie. Her pedigree was quite an outcross (bearing in mind that Weimaraners were only allowed out of Germany in the early 1950s).

ARE DOGS BETTER TODAY?

Breeds have improved enormously as regards health, through better nutrition and knowledge, in the same way that people have. Coats have become longer and stronger because shampoos and supplements in feed have become so much more sophisticated; furthermore owners and handlers are so professional in presentation: it is an art form to see the skilled groomers at work. They are as professionally trained as the top hairdressers, and many compete for awards at the highest level. Years ago it was generally the *bona fide* professional handlers who were eloquent in the art of preparing a dog, and these handlers were often confined to the terrier men, who, it must be said, are today just as skilled as their predecessors.

A valid point to be made, is the fact that cameras have become so much more technical, therefore producing quality reproductions. What have cameras got to do with dog breeding? Old photos gave a more distorted view of the subject, so the dog in the scratchy black and white snap was not a true image of what he actually looked like.

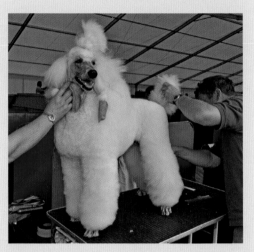

Grooming is essential for the wellbeing of the dog, particularly in long-coated breeds.

Annie was in turn mated to another dog, Cirrus, which was not closely related, but had redeeming attributes. This union produced Harry. All had exemplary temperaments. We took advice from people who studied genetics, deliberated long and hard, and as a result mated Annie back to her son Harry. Ten puppies were born, all like peas in a pod, and more importantly with no obvious genetic problems. We retained Joy, who became the basis of our 'line'. Interestingly, Joy is still the champion-producing, record-holding brood bitch in the breed today.

Joy was mated to another, unrelated American import; the pedigree details are shown on page 73.

Study of the pedigrees used as examples here show how we have used outcrosses to prevent the line stagnating; soundness in body and mind, plus type, has always prioritized our breeding programme.

However successful a kennel is at producing top dogs, the majority of puppies produced will live in a home with a family who may not have lived with the breed before. It is paramount that breeding programmes should take this fact into account: our ethos reflects this, and so should yours.

The size of the gene pool can be enlarged more easily these days due to the introduction of pet passports: this means that it is an easy matter, and with

Breed : Weimaraner
Sex : Bitch
Date Of Birth :
Breeder :
Owner :
Kennel Club Number :

Pedigree Of
Gunalt Joy

13-Sep-10

Colour: Silver Grey

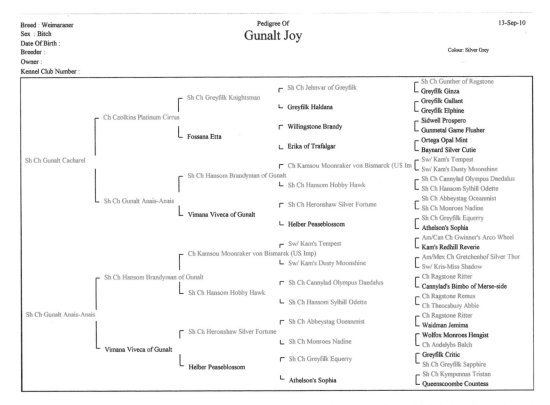

The pedigree of Gunalt Joy, top champion-producing Weimaraner brood bitch in UK, and top brood bitch all breeds in 1995.

no added stress to the bitch, to take her by car over to Europe or beyond to use a dog, thereby introducing new blood. We also have proficient vets who are now specializing in fertility and the science of artificial insemination, and the import and export of frozen semen.

INHERITED AND CONGENITAL PROBLEMS

People frequently confuse 'congenital' and 'inherited': inherited means 'acquired genetically from the parents'; 'congenital' means 'present at birth'. Congenital problems can arise through genetic influences, but they are usually

MUTATION

Sometimes a gene may be adapted by mutation. Left to nature, this mutation could be the start of a new species, however this would only occur if the mutated species were to fit into the environment naturally, having gained a strength during its mutation, which would prove advantageous for its future; otherwise it would die out, rather in terms of 'the survival of the fittest'.

Epistasis – meaning that genes can mask and alter the effects of other genes – is different from mutation and accounts for the mechanism behind more complex polygenic conditions.

developmental, whereas many inherited diseases are not obvious until the animal starts to mature – which is exactly why we have trouble getting rid of them!

Cryptorchism and Monorchism

Conditions that are congenital, and fairly certainly hereditary, are cryptorchism and monorchism. 'Cryptorchid' comes from the Greek words *kryptos* meaning 'hidden', 'secret' or 'covered', and orchid referring to the testicles. The term 'monorchid' is not altogether correct (meaning one testicle only), as usually both testicles are present in the body but only one is noticeable in the scrotum: therefore the more correct term is 'unilateral cryptorchid'.

Normally a tube runs from the inner lining of the abdomen to the scrotum. Inside the tube are the spermatic cord, artery, vein, nerves, vas deferens and the cremaster muscle. The muscle is there to pull the testicles closer to the body in cold conditions and to allow them to hang lower in the scrotum when the weather is warmer. In the abdominal wall there is a ring-like passage known as the inguinal ring, and the testicles move through this ring some time after birth. In cryptorchism, one or both testicles stay inside the tube, often because the opening of the inguinal ring is not big enough for them to pass through. Some testicles may pass through the ring later. Most testicles are generally down in the scrotum before the dog is about four months of age; if they are not descended into the scrotum by the age of eight months, they would usually be classed as retained. In this case castration would be advisable, though your vet would be sure to wait until the dog was at least eight months to ensure they were not likely to descend on their own.

The most common reason for retained testicles is that the spermatic cord is too short, due to a genetic defect. Therefore the dog should not be used at stud, perpetuating the condition in progeny.

It is unlikely that a bilateral cryptorchid dog would have viable sperm, as retained testicles are at temperature that is 4–5° higher than is conducive for the production of testosterone. A monorchid or unilateral cryptorchid is still able to produce puppies, from the one testicle that is present in the scrotum.

When retained, the testicles are at a much higher risk of sertoli cell tumours. (The sertoli cell in the testicle provides nourishment to the sperm cells.) If this form of tumour occurs it is prone to be malignant.

In rare instances, but possible in cryptorchids, torsion (twisting) of the spermatic cord may occur.

Thus monorchism/cryptorchism brings an increased risk of several health problems; consequently if this condition is apparent, castration is advisable.

Hip Dysplasia

Hip dysplasia is a phenotype, meaning that it is the characteristic/trait that you see. It is a multifactorial condition, which has a genetic component but also many environmental influences. Study has shown that if the parent is suffering from the condition, the offspring will have a higher chance of being afflicted. Nutrition deficiencies can contribute to this condition, namely lack of sufficient calcium and protein. Calcium is the main component of bones, and protein is the building block for muscles, which support bones. Because large breeds grow more quickly, deficiencies are more likely and forces are more dramatic, making large breeds more vulnerable to bone and joint problems. Over-feeding of the young animal can cause joints to grow abnormally, particularly the ball and socket joints of the hips, thereby putting too much pressure on growing joints.

Moreover too much intense and excessive exercise in growing youngsters, when bones are developing, can also affect the hip and other joint development.

In Summary

Multifactorial and polygenic problems are not so easy to trace or eradicate, as many of the exact genes are still not known. It is to be hoped that with the progression of mapping the genome of different breeds of dogs, this is something that will become much easier in the future.

Obviously it would not be possible to fill the whole of this book on health, hereditary or congenital matters, so just a few examples have been given here, which are relevant to genetic topics.

Before embarking on your chosen breed, it is easy to do some research on it through the Kennel Club on the internet, and talk over any inherent problems, which could be applicable to the breed in question, with enthusiasts.

ABOVE: The vet may refer a dog with joint problems to a hydrotherapy centre for treatment. Hydrotherapy can alleviate pain and re-introduce mobility.

RIGHT: The water treadmill has heated, cleansed water, to relieve pounding as the dog walks. The glass walls allow the operator to see exact footfall, thus aiding rehabilitation.

4 THE BROOD BITCH

Having a brood bitch and subsequently breeding from her categorizes the owner as a breeder. In effect anyone who reproduces plants or animals is classed as a breeder. There are conscientious breeders and those who breed for profit. So what gives one person the right to be a breeder of anything, and another not?

POSITIVE BREEDING

When people start breeding, it is usually as a result of acquiring a bitch as a pet. Then they become involved in showing, and from there have the desire to produce a litter of puppies, generally because they want to keep a puppy so as to be able to show a dog they have bred.

It must be remembered that the bitch you start with will always have the ability to influence your future 'line'. So if you bought your bitch as a pet and she is just a 'nice' bitch, lacking type and without any redeeming qualities, it may be worth looking at top winning kennels in the breed of your interest. If you express an interest in showing and breeding the owners will try to help you – after all, it is for the good of the future of the breed if they help you acquire an excellence example with which to procreate the breed.

We started showing with an English Setter bought as a pet. A sound enough bitch, she was a little plain in the head and also had a low tail-set. Twenty years later, we could still see those issues in an occasional puppy.

These Pharaoh Hounds – mother and son – prove that quality produces quality.

Hobby Breeding

Hobby breeders are those who decide to have a litter or litters because they think their bitch is so lovely that it would be just delightful to have a puppy related to her. They are still breeders, and why should they not have a litter from their bitch, any more than someone who consistently produces champions? The responsibility and dedication should be the same for both 'breeders'. And if the 'hobby breeder' inquires about using an eminent stud dog, as long as they have made an honest, critical appraisal of their bitch and fulfilled health checks, all ought to be well.

The fanciful conception of breeding from the family pet is that since she is so sweet in nature and pretty, she will reproduce puppies in the same mould. What is more, the adult members of the family might feel that having a litter will instil positive sex education in the children. In an ideal world the puppies will be born on white fluffy bedding at half-hour intervals. The dam will clean the whelps, and all will suckle and grow fat and bonny.

Experienced breeders are aware that this scenario is not always the case. The litter might consist of one dead puppy born by Caesarean section – although a rare occurrence, this can happen, and would cause real upset to all the family. The monetary costs would be high – vet's fees and stud fees are not cheap. On the other hand, the dam could produce eight or ten puppies without any trouble – which sounds great, but there is still a down side: this number of ten-week-old puppies would require an enormous amount of time to look after. Feeding and cleaning out is a never-ending task, and they all compete for attention, making it impossible to socialize each

Playful eight-week-old puppies can take up an enormous amount of time.

puppy decently. Furthermore all must be found homes. Again the stress on the family is extensive.

Retaining a number of puppies from a litter is hardly fair to the puppies. From eight weeks old a puppy needs individual attention in order to thrive and develop. Initially managing the puppies may seem easy as they play together; however, as they increase in physical and mental maturity, peer pressure will become apparent. In adolescence, fighting could arise because they are vying for pecking order. If two or more bitches of the same age are kept, they will tend to bring each other into season – and hormones increase irritability, so quarrels start.

In breeding kennels with many bitches, it is an accepted fact that they will bring each other into season. If all are differing ages, a pecking order will already have been established so problems are less likely to crop up. Nevertheless it is prudent to be extra watchful during this time, just in case tempers flare. We had a bitch that two weeks before her season would develop a 'furrowed brow': providing she was left alone by the other dogs, peace reigned – but if playing youngsters bumped into her, they were quickly reprimanded!

CHOOSING THE BREED

It cannot be stressed enough that when embarking on breeding – whatever the animal, but in this case dogs – you should always choose for your foundation stock the healthiest, most soundly constructed dog, one that typifies the breed. It is the breeder's responsibility to the future of the breed and to those who buy the resulting puppies that the breed is reproduced and reared according to the highest standards.

People usually choose a breed of dog because it appeals to them, in much the same way as they might select their partner. And because as a breeder you are the custodian of that breed, selecting the breed that suits you is important. It is also essential that you are aware of how the breed will fit into a normal family environment, as most of the puppies you breed will become family pets. Even the most successful breeders of quality dogs that win in a working or show situation will only have a limited number of puppies with enough potential for competition.

The following points should be considered when breeding and homing puppies:

• Will the breed be biddable? The breed

The breeder relies on vision to assess the puppy's potential and knowledge of its ancestors to decide if it has prospective worth for breeding and showing/working ability.

Waiting for a promising puppy pays dividends.

temperament traits must be taken into consideration: for example, hounds tend to go off hunting; some breeds are habitually destructive.

- Will the breed be tolerant of children?
- Will the breed need exceptional requirements, for example grooming, exercise?

Researching the breed of your choice is essential. Breed books are available on most breeds, giving their requirements. Speak to breeders and check their credibility with the Kennel Club. Remember, beauty is in the eye of the beholder, so the breeder will extol the virtues of their own dogs, which may not in fact be as accurate as they think.

So you have chosen the breed: now you need to obtain a puppy. If you want to breed dogs, you will have to select a bitch puppy: this will be the foundation of your 'line'. If you have a female you can select the stud dog that will complement and further the qualities you are looking for; if you choose a male, you are limited as to who wishes to use the dog. First rate, established breeders will have a good record of dogs that are winning, and therefore conforming to the standard of the breed, and they will be happy to offer support. Often you will have to be patient because there will be a waiting list for puppies from breeders with a good reputation.

When you have your puppy, she should be reared with decent food as befitting her requirements, also with love and socialization. This will make for a confident, contented bitch, which is a good foundation to start from. Make sure that all breeding stock is health checked.

Researching your Chosen Breed

There is a theory prevalent amongst the uninformed media that dog showing is to the detriment of dogs. In fact it is quite the opposite: it may appear a 'beauty contest', but it gives breeders first-hand knowledge of the stock that is being produced, which in turn means that breeders can breed better dogs. Likewise field trails will tell you if the dogs produced still retain the instinct for which they were originally developed – hunting, pointing and retrieving – and the same applies for hounds and herding dogs. These things are inherent and cannot be put there with training alone if the dog's natural ability has been lost through ignorant breeding.

Enthusiasts devote a great deal of time, money and effort to participate in this 'sport' of showing, and why would they go to these great lengths if it were not for the love of their breed? From the dogs in the show ring observers can see for themselves the temperament of a particular kennel and that of the progeny of stud dogs. Family traits can be monitored. Dogs can be studied visually, and not just on hearsay.

If you have a clear view of the progeny produced by a kennel it will make it much easier for you to build a foundation for your 'line'.

Bitches Fit to Breed From

Whilst in theory a bitch could be bred from every time she comes in season (if she is in a fit enough condition for nature to allow this), starting from her very first one, the universal feeling is that this would be unethical. Generally the unwritten rule is about three or four litters from one bitch in her lifetime, since the welfare of the bitch, as well as

These Foxhounds are showing their natural instinct to perform inherent traits.

To produce a bright healthy puppy is so rewarding.

the breed, should be at the heart of all caring breeders.

If a bitch consistently produces quality puppies, it is not unusual to breed her to a fourth litter. However, we had a bitch that had a sound, healthy litter, with each new owner entirely satisfied with their lovely new acquisition, yet we felt the puppies lacked the desired type and so we had her neutered. We felt that we were not going forward with breeding from that particular bitch.

Obviously, all breeding stock should be screened for any hereditary conditions attaining to the breed; they should also be permanently identifiable. There are different ways of achieving this. Dogs can be tattooed, usually in the earflap. The Kennel Club runs a scheme to collect DNA samples from dogs, which is a way of identifying individual dogs. The DNA is the assessment of a dog's genetic make-up and ancestry. This is also a way of pinpointing some hereditary conditions.

The most common trend these days is to microchip the dog because it is easy to scan him so as to check his identity in the event of him being lost, or for Kennel Club ID. On the negative side it is thought that the chip can migrate, which makes scanning difficult; however this rarely happens, and if he is chipped when he is over four months of age it is even less likely to happen. Younger puppies tend to have a lot of loose skin, especially in larger breeds, and it is thought this is one reason why the chip might move about.

However punctilious you are in fulfilling all these requirements, it will not automatically make you a good breeder. Some people never produce more than one or two excellent specimens, and often it is just a great amount of natural instinct and a talent for animal husbandry that sets some breeders apart. However, if you are honest and devoted to your task, that is all anyone can ask.

THE BITCH'S REPRODUCTIVE SYSTEM

The eggs are produced in the ovaries, of which there are two, encased in a protective shield. The Fallopian tubes connect the ovaries to the horns of the uterus, which are identical. Full-term puppies will pass from the uterus, through the cervix, then through the vagina and into the big world out of the vulva. The whole reproductive system is made up of soft tissue, so that following fertilization, the tissues can stretch and grow to accommodate the developing puppies.

The bladder lies on the underside of the uterus with the urethra, which takes out urine through a parallel cylinder by means of the vulva.

If any of the soft tissue passes through the pelvic girdle it can cause a blockage when a puppy is being whelped.

The pelvis is made up of three fused bones: the pubis, the ischium and the ilium. In short-legged breeds the pelvic bones tend to be equal in width to height; in larger breeds with long legs the pelvic cavity is higher than it is wide, which tends to allow easier whelping. In breeds where the pelvis is almost vertical, this can cause difficulties in whelping, as the puppy has to negotiate the pubis to be born.

Because these bones fuse as the bitch reaches full maturity, it is often advisable to breed from her earlier rather than later. Some smaller breeds – toy breeds and small terrier breeds – will be mated at eighteen months of age. Generally the optimum time is the second or third season, or the season after the bitch is two years old. We would not advise a first litter from a bitch at five years old, except on a vet's recommendation; nor would we condone breeding from her on her first season.

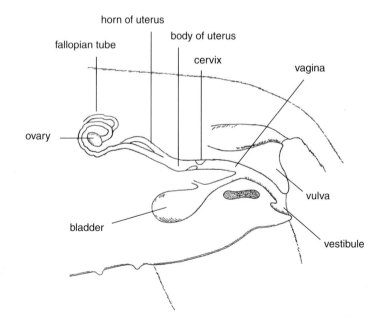

The reproductive system of the bitch.

Bitches who live together often bring each other into season.

The Reproductive Cycle

A bitch can come into season from about six months of age, though it is more likely that she will have her first season at approximately twelve months of age. If she has not had her first season by the time she is over eighteen months of age, it may be worth consulting the vet for advice.

'The book' says a bitch will have a season every six months, which in principle is all right, but in practice each one is different. During her first two years her seasons may be erratic, though ultimately they are more inclined to settle into a pattern of around the accepted six-month cycle. We have known bitches that have their season every four months, which can be tedious; however, following the first litter the cycle conforms to more regular conduct. On the other hand, some bitches only have a season every twelve or eighteen months, so catching this bitch and mating her successfully can be more complicated. If she does not conceive on a couple of occasions of being mated, she could be too old to have puppies before she has even had one litter.

LICENCES

A breeder who has three or more breeding bitches, either living at the premises or at another establishment, must have a breeding licence; this is issued by the local environmental health department of the local government, and is implemented in accordance with the Breeding of Dogs Act 1973, revised in 1999. Principally it gives the following recommendations:

- Accommodation must be suitable in size, relating to the breed and the numbers kept.
- The dogs' housing must be of suitable construction so that it cannot be chewed, and can be cleaned adequately to avoid the build-up of infectious and contagious diseases.
- The housing should be such that in case of emergency or fire the animals can be brought out safely.
- Lighting, temperature and ventilation must be sufficient for the dogs' comfort and wellbeing.
- The dogs must be fed properly, and have access to fresh water and sufficient bedding.
- They should be given enough exercise as would be applicable for their welfare.
- Bitches should not have more than six litters in their lifetime.
- They must not be mated to produce a litter at less than one year of age.
- They must not produce a litter within one year of the date of birth of the previous litter.
- Records must be kept of each bitch, including all aspects of identification and inoculations, plus all records relating to seasons, whelping and puppies.

For the application of the breeding licence and a full list of regulations, look under the Breeding of Dogs Act 1973 on your pc. A delegate of the local authority will inspect your premises yearly.

THE IMPORTANCE OF KEEPING RECORDS

Records pertaining to each bitch should contain the data of health check results, her seasons, and any whelping information; this will also help with any future breeding plans. It is so easy to forget pertinent information, so record details meticulously; it will serve you well in the long run. Make a note of when inoculations are given, her worming programme and flea prevention treatment: it is so easy to forget these simple yet necessary management responsibilities.

If you record when a bitch comes into season, when she goes out of 'colour' and when she turns her tail and is therefore receptive to the dog, when you do decide to mate her it will take much of the guesswork out of the mating programme.

A bitch can have her season suppressed with an injection of progestagen, administered by a vet. However, there is a very small risk that this could stop her ever coming into season again. Also there is a slightly raised chance of womb infection (pyometra). Likewise, if a bitch is accidentally mismated, the vet can stop conception by administering a female hormone drug, given on days three and five after the mating. Again this can induce problems, so if drugs can be avoided it is an advantage.

All these details are recorded for future reference. We have a folder file for each bitch, and these records are retained. It makes interesting reading, looking back over the years, how family traits are passed on – proving nature over nurture.

THE BITCH'S REPRODUCTIVE PHASE

We use the term 'season' or 'heat' to describe when a bitch will be able to reproduce, i.e. when she releases eggs into her womb.

Bitches generally come into season in

The oestrus cycle, which may be as short as four months or as long as twelve.

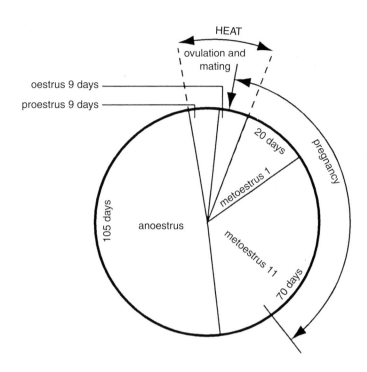

spring and autumn, as is often the case with many animals – spring when all wakes up, buds grow on plants, birds migrate back after the winter. Puppies are born in late spring/ early summer, and by the time they are ready to go the nights are drawing shorter, the days a little warmer. People think of having a new puppy when they can let it out to housetrain it, and can take it for walks. In high summer, people think of holidays – in mid-winter they are saving for Christmas, so a new puppy is not their first thought. (Besides, it is to be hoped that no one wants to breed a puppy for Christmas, as no one should want to buy a puppy for Christmas!)

So how do you know when your bitch is ready to be mated? The bitch's reproductive phase forms four parts throughout the yearly cycle: anoestrus, pre-oestrus, oestrus and metoestrus.

Anoestrus
Anoestrus is the quiet time when the bitch is not attractive or attracted to males. It is the time between seasons when her hormones are calm.

Pro-Oestrus
When a bitch is in pre-oestrus she is experiencing an increase in oestrogen levels; this is commonly known as 'coming into season'. Often she will show signs of coming into season up to two weeks before she actually shows 'colour': she can appear moody or grumpy, and she may often squat to wee. As time goes on her vulva will swell, and dogs may start to show interest in her, even though she is not bleeding (known as 'being in colour') or fertile at this time.

As the pro-oestrus continues her vulva will become quite swollen and red, and will discharge spots of clear red blood.

Often during the first season the young bitch is not fully aware of what is happening and does not clean her vulva sufficiently, so if she lives in the home the discharge will stain carpets and soft furniture. Some owners devise amazing ways of staunching the discharge – I have seen bitches with an old T-shirt or pair of knickers tied to their hindquarters to stop the blood! Subsequent seasons don't generally cause the same problem, as she is more experienced in cleanliness.

It is also possible that a bitch has a 'silent season', which means that the vulva does not swell excessively and there is little or no evidence of colour. It is not really understood why this occurs; the only indication of being in season is that the bitch may show signs of flirting with other bitches or males.

Oestrus

Oestrus is the time when the bitch is most receptive to the male and can conceive. The vulva becomes quite swollen and large (to accept the male's penis), and is quite warm to the touch (this is probably where the term 'on heat' comes from). This is usually between about the eleventh and fourteenth days of her season, counting from when the first spots of blood are seen.

Of course, nature and living things don't always conform to the 'book', and I have known a bitch that conceived on the first day of colour (she was owned by an experienced breeder, so was not overlooked), and another that had a litter of nine puppies after she was mated on her twenty-third day in season. We had a bitch which actually conceived when

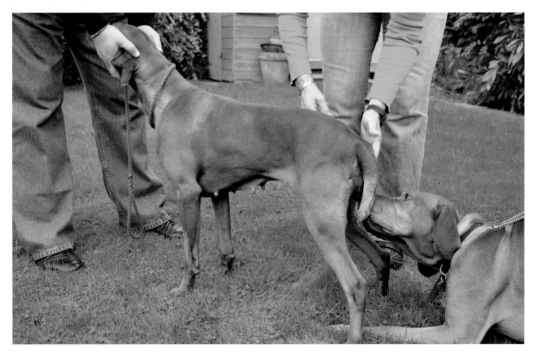

This bitch is ready for mating; the dog licks her vulva to stimulate her to accept him mating her.

mated on her twelfth day in season, yet would 'stand' happily for a dog and allow him to mate with her on the twenty-eighth day; fortunately she never had puppies on these second occasions. Nevertheless, it was a tiresome habit.

When the bitch is ready to be mated she will 'stand', when she will back up to the dog (or another bitch, cat, you, or even the furniture, if no male is available!). To see if she is receptive, before introducing the stud dog, run your fingers firmly from the root of her tail up her back; if she is ready, she will arch her back and throw her tail to one side over her back. Each breed can have different traits, but this is generally a useful sign that she is getting ready. After a day or two of doing this, she will become more exaggerated in her display; this is when she will be ready to mate.

Blood tests can be done at two-day intervals, which gives more definite evidence of ovulation. Alternatively the bitch can be swabbed (see vaginal cytology, below). Both these procedures will require veterinary intervention, so she will have to be taken to the surgery every other day of her season. The blood sample will be sent to the laboratory for analysis, and when the optimum time arrives for mating she will have to be taken to the dog within possibly twelve hours. This means that forward planning is crucial; also the veterinary costs must be taken into account. Nor is this method of calculating ovulation foolproof.

If a natural mating fails to secure pregnancy the first time, it might be worth considering veterinary intervention the next time.

During oestrus, compounds commonly known as pheromones are emitted from the vagina. These are airborne chemicals and are carried far and wide, thus attract-ing males from long distances, indicating that the bitch is receptive for mating.

Metoestrus
Metoestrus is the final stage of the cycle; this occurs following the bitch's season if she has not been mated, or if she failed to become pregnant. Hormone changes cause the bitch to develop signs that she is in whelp, both in the way she behaves and physically, convincing the breeder that she will produce puppies, until it is obvious that she has not conceived. This can be very deflating for both bitch and owner, as everything will have been prepared for the impending birth. This is commonly called phantom pregnancy, also known as false or pseudo pregnancy.

The bitch does everything to suggest that she is indeed pregnant. At three weeks' gestation she will not eat as normal, but will become picky with her food; she may put on weight and steady up in her activity. As the weeks progress she will start to dig holes in the garden, preparing, in her mind, where she will have her puppies. However, usually by week eight of gestation she will deflate, and it is obvious that she is not in whelp. Nevertheless, at full term she will gather a toy to 'nurse', and may even come into milk.

These symptoms could well be a legacy from many years ago when dogs lived wild, in the pack, when the alpha bitch might avail herself of a 'nanny bitch', which could feed puppies born to the alpha bitch without actually whelping herself.

If a bitch suffers a severe false pregnancy it is wise to take her thoughts away from puppies. Increase her exercise and activity to give her something else to think about, and if she has been fed as if she were in whelp, decrease the amount

The bitch shows a raised backbone as her puppies are taking nutrients from her. This is a sure sign of pregnancy; in a false pregnancy a bitch might 'balloon', but would not lose condition over the spine.

of food. Don't let her have toys, especially squeaky ones, as this will amplify the problem.

If she is lactating, reduce her consumption of water so that the milk glands have a chance to dry up. Check to make sure the glands do not become hot and hard, which could mean she is developing mastitis. Because there is no expulsion the mammary glands will generally dry up naturally.

COMMON HEALTH CONCERNS AND CONDITIONS

Ovarian Imbalance

Alternatively this condition goes by the name of endocrine dermatosis. It is caused by abnormalities of ovarian function in bitches, and there are two types:

- Type 1 is linked with functional ovarian tumours or cystic ovaries, and consists of bilateral symmetrical alopecia, each side of the loin. Symptoms include gynecomastia, which is an enlarged vulva, and abnormalities of the oestrus cycle.
- Type 2 is a bilaterally symmetrical alopecia, often with seborrhoea, in spayed bitches. This can respond to treatment with oestrogen. The condition is otherwise called oestrogen-responsive dermatosis.

Hyperthyroidism

The main symptom of this condition is the lack of the thyroid hormone secretion. This can affect the bitch's fertility and cause an irregular oestrous cycle. Even if the bitch conceives, there is a strong possibility of reabsorption of the foetuses. Signs will also include lethargy, dull coat and colour change. Veterinarian treatment of thyroxin can be successful. This condition is rare in dogs, so don't assume that failure to establish pregnancy in a bitch is due to this.

Vaginal Cytology

Vaginal cytology is a clinical way of assessing the optimum time to mate the bitch. It can also be used to detect infections in the vagina. A vet would perform this procedure as proficiency is needed in gaining a correct reading, so it involves time and travel to the surgery.

The vet inserts a cotton swab through the vulva into the vagina. When the swab reaches the urethral orifice, it is rotated to gather the cells. These cells are tested, giving an accurate reading of when the bitch is in oestrus and therefore ready for mating.

Some bitches will show signs of flirting even when not in oestrus, so for maximum chance of conception it is best to start vaginal cytology within two to three days of bleeding in case the bitch ovulates early. The procedure should be performed every two days throughout the timing process.

As the bitch progresses through pro-oestrus the cell types visualized on the cytology slides will change: under the influence of oestrogen, the vaginal epithelium thickens. The slide from the early pro-oestrus period is similar to the metoestrus slide, which is why the test must be done at two-day intervals. The swab must be passed as far into the vagina as possible to give a clearer indication of the hormonal changes.

Just as the cell type changes, so does the appearance of the vaginal epithelium. In pre-oestrus the tissue of the vagina is evenly pink and swollen. Early oestrus the vaginal wall starts to dry out and the flow of blood subsides. This results in the vaginal wall becoming paler in colour until it is white, the tissue appearing wrinkly when fully in oestrus and ready for mating. Once past ovulation the walls of the vagina become blotchy pink and red.

Following ovulation it takes the eggs two days to mature and be ready for fertilization, and there is a three- to four-day window when fertilization can take place. This is the reason that many people will want to mate a bitch more than once, with an interval of two days.

Pyometra

We have touched on inflammation of the womb, or pyometra. The bitch will have a foul-smelling, sludgy pinkish discharge; she will drink excessively and appear depressed. However, if she has a closed pyometra the signs are not always easy to spot, but if veterinary intervention is not swift, you will be in danger of losing the bitch. Toxins are released from the infection into the bloodstream, making the bitch very ill; eventually these toxins can cause liver failure. The vet will often want to give antibiotics for twelve to twenty-four hours before surgery. Generally the bitch will need to have the infected womb removed.

Occasionally (and if caught early enough) special hormone injections may be given to empty the womb, although this is not often a successful solution.

This condition in very old animals presents clear evidence of organ failure – kidney and liver failure and heart disease – and perhaps euthanasia may be the kindest option.

This is the reason that when a bitch has had her three litters, and/or reached an age when we would not wish to breed her again (usually about seven years) we would have the bitch spayed, removing any chance of pyometra in later life.

BOOKING THE STUD DOG

Of course you cannot have a brood bitch unless you have a stud dog, otherwise she is purely a bitch by definition. If one wants to be pernickety you could work on the premise of using artificial insemination, known as AI; this will be covered in the chapter about the stud dog.

Always research the dogs that are pleasing to you. Watch his progeny, how they grow on, is he consistently producing offspring that reflect his qualities to bitches similar in stature and lineage to the bitch you have. You may draw up a shortlist of dogs that appeal. You will want a copy of the relevant pedigrees of such males to compare with your bitch's pedigree. It must be stressed to the owners of these males that you would like to have a copy of the pedigree but you are only enquiring at this stage, and not booking the dog as the stud for your bitch. If this is not made clear, you will antagonize the owners of stud dogs, and you will probably then be unable to use the dog, if he is ultimately your choice. In fact word will travel that you are a time waster.

If you treat people with respect, the same will be reciprocated. It is wise to ask for help from the breeder of your bitch, as they will recognize which lines complement each other.

On confirmation of the stud dog you wish to use, book him well before the bitch is in season. Enquire about terms, whether they want a stud fee or a puppy; is there a free repeat if the bitch 'misses' the first time; will the stud owner be able to help secure enquiries for puppies – so that everything is clear and preparation is in place.

Check through your records of when the bitch is standing for mating so that you can give an approximation of when you will need to go to the stud. If you are a beginner and your bitch a maiden (term used for a bitch who has not been mated before), you may need to go a little earlier, which will allow the more experienced stud owner to gauge the timing of the mating. Obviously this is unacceptable if travelling great distances, but can be useful if the stud is local.

When the first spots of blood appear confirming her season has started, contact the stud owner. It does not bode well to have a phone call from a bitch owner saying that they would be along tomorrow as the bitch is ready for mating. Stud dog owners have lives too!

5 THE STUD DOG

A breeder usually starts his breeding enterprise with a bitch, and may then keep a dog from the first litter. Of course you could have a male dog from the start, which when seen in competition – be it the show ring, hunting field, or agility or obedience classes – is noticed for his merit. Then his breeder may ask to use him for his lines, and so he becomes a stud dog. If he produces quality offspring there is a distinct probability that more enquiries will be made about him as a stud.

It is naive or misguided to assume that obtaining a male puppy and expecting him to become a stud is a viable proposition unless he grows into a fine specimen of his breed, and is shown in an environment where he can be publicly observed.

There is always a possibility that someone will contact you because they have discovered that you have a male of the breed and they have a bitch. Be wary: why would someone want to use a dog that is not known or seen unless they thought he were local or cheap! This is not the way to breed dogs!

Remember, if you have a stud dog, you too have a responsibility to the resulting puppies. Breed clubs have a code of conduct, and nearly all have a rescue/rehoming scheme, and will call upon the

This Labrador is a lovely pet but does not have redeeming qualities to pass on.

stud dog owner if puppies 'bounce' (come up for rehoming).

If you are going to use your dog at stud you must be honest. Has he redeeming qualities to pass on? These will be easier to assess if the potential stud dog is seen; thus owners looking for a compatible male to mate to their bitch will inquire about a dog's availability when they see him at a show in the ring, a field trial or in agility or obedience classes – at least used in some way.

SOUNDNESS

It is important that the stud dog is physically and mentally sound – fit and healthy in body and in mind. The following aspects should be studied when making a judgement on a stud dog:

Conformation: Make and shape is important for both the male and the female. A quality animal is judged by his appearance, and requires above all a sound construction (*see* Chapter 3).

Balance: Being in balance means that each part works in harmony, and the dog's conformation is of complementary proportions throughout, therefore allowing fluid freedom of movement without putting undue strain on any joints.

Type: The dog should have the look applicable to his function, hence giving him type. He has been bred, often for hundreds of years, in such a way that he can perform his occupation, and can therefore fulfil his breed requirements – the purpose for his existence – in the most efficient way.

Style: This is the way in which the dog presents himself. He should be confident about the task in hand. One of the most

Nora is the top winning Chinese Crested: her sound, balanced construction is easy to see, even to the untrained eye.

A really good quality dog.

loathsome tendencies in a dog is nervousness. With this trait a dog is more likely to bite first and ask questions later, out of fear, leading to unpredictability. A confident guarding breed is not going to bite if he is trained properly, only warn or go forwards under instruction. So a nervous or insecure dog should never be bred from, as this genetic mannerism will come through, if not in the first generation then certainly in subsequent ones.

When all these attributes are apparent, the dog will present a picture of quality. This is evident in all animals, and furthermore, not only does something generally perform better if it has these attributes, it also has a longer life – and this is true of cars, clothes and most living things.

THE STUD DOG OWNER'S RESPONSIBILITY

An enquiry has been made as to the availability of your dog at stud. Your dog has had all the necessary health checks and these have been submitted to the appropriate authority, with satisfactory results. You also have a responsibility to make sure the bitch has successfully completed all relevant screening programmes. This is not only for the future good of the breed and proof that you are professional in your manner: you are also safeguarding yourself against potential future problems, since nowadays so many people seem to operate from a 'where there's blame there's a claim' standpoint.

LICENSING PREREQUISITES IN GERMANY

In some countries dogs can only be used for breeding if they are licensed. For example in Germany, a German Shepherd Dog has to pass the breed survey (*Korung* in German), indicated by KKL1 or KKL2, which will appear after the dog's name and titles. This requires demanding examinations of the dog in order to pass him as suitable for breeding.

He is tested for temperament; gun sensitivity will be tested for protection capabilities. He must demonstrate sound nerve by passing BH obedience and temperament tests. He should be titled *Schutzhund*, which can take months or years of training in tracking and obedience. Hips are scored: they must be OFA certified or A stamped. He is obliged to pass an AD test (*Ausdauerprüfung* or Endurance Test) demonstrating physical soundness by running over twelve miles at the side of the handler on a bicycle.

He is tattooed and is required to have a show rating of at least G (good) at a German conformation show. The breed survey master will also note pigment, coat, eye and toenail colour as well as conformation and size.

The highest grade a dog can gain is KKL1 'highly recommended for breeding', then KKL2 'suitable for breeding', or he will be totally ineligible. If he has one or two missing teeth, despite passing every other requirement, he can only gain KKL2; any more missing teeth and he will be ineligible.

The German Shepherd Dog has had bad press for being bred with so-called exaggerations; this one, however, is obviously sound and balanced. (Photo: Lisa Croft-Elliott)

The stud dog can only pass on redeeming qualities if he possesses them, as can the dam. It is therefore a wise move to invite the bitch's owner to bring her to visit, so that you can assess both her merits and her owner's approach to breeding. Many a stud dog owner has been holding the dogs whilst they are tied and absent-minded, and has just glanced, say, in the bitch's mouth, to find that her bite is incorrect. Needless to say, at this point it is too late to refuse to allow your dog to mate with her.

If you allow your dog to be used on a mediocre bitch, or worse still a bitch with inherent defects, it will reflect badly on the dog if the resulting litter has the same faults, and could mean that people lose interest in him for stud work. Astute breeders and stud dog owners learn early on that the breed is only as good as the stock it is bred from. If untypical, unsound stock is used for breeding, these dogs are for ever in the pedigree, and capable of being reproduced. It also seems to be true that if beautiful puppies

The bitch can easily rear a large number of healthy puppies.

are produced, the dam is given the credit; but if the puppies are sub-standard or showing hereditary faults, it is usually the sire that is blamed.

We feel it obligatory to stress the reasons for breeding, and what is likely to become of puppies if suitable homes are not forthcoming.

PAYMENT OF STUD FEES

Stud fees and terms must be clearly laid out. It was always an unwritten rule that the first time a dog was used, there would be no fee, as the dog was being 'proved'. Would he produce puppies? Would they be up to standard in character and soundness? However, because the price of puppies has escalated, not to pay anything is often considered unfair these days, so it is usual that a reduced stud fee is paid when the litter is born.

When a dog is 'proven' the stud fee will increase. Furthermore, when the dog has won titles of excellence, and has proved that the puppies he sires are of the same order, whether in the field or the show ring, then his fee will rise again.

How much the stud fee will be will differ between breeds. Many breeds currently charge a fee which is the same as the price of a puppy. Some kennels will charge a handling fee and an agreed amount per puppy on parturition of the whelps.

It must be decided before mating when the fee is to be paid. The most likely time

This top winning Standard Poodle, owned by Mike Gadsby and Jason Lynn, has also sired champion puppies. (Photo: Lisa Croft-Elliott)

is on completion of mating, when the bitch owner will be furnished with a receipt, a pedigree, and the kennel club registration form, filled in with the name of the sire, his registration number, the date of mating, and the signature of the owner/s of the sire.

The brood bitch owner retains this until parturition, when it can be completed with details of the dam, the date of birth, the names of the puppies, and so on. It is then returned to the Kennel Club with the relevant fee to register the litter.

A fine example of a fit and sound stud dog.

If it is agreed that the stud fee will be paid on completion of whelping, the Kennel Club form will not be given or signed until the stud fee is paid. This method of payment is usually agreed because the stud dog may be aged or he has missed getting a few bitches in whelp, and it is in doubt as to whether he is producing enough strong, active sperm.

In a fit, healthy stud that is producing fine puppies, you will be charging for the service of the stud, and not necessarily puppies, because it is likely to be the bitch's fault if she misses. This is the main reason that stud fees are not refundable. The stud owner may make a proviso that if there are no puppies the bitch can have a free return. Again, this must be clearly set out at the start of inquiries. If the stud owner has more than one stud dog, it can be the case that another dog will be available to use if the bitch fails to conceive; however, this is by no means a definite.

The contract between bitch and stud owners may have the stipulation that the stud owner will take a puppy instead of a fee. In this case it must be made absolutely clear whether the puppy that is to be received in place of the fee will be a dog or a bitch, first pick or subse-

quent, and if any colour or marking is desired as a preference.

There is always the possibility that only one puppy is whelped, in which case it must be agreed in advance whether settlement will be fee or ownership – likewise if a bitch is scanned and proved to be in whelp, but then absorbs the litter. If the bitch delivers a litter but the puppies are all dead, or she has one dead puppy born by Caesarean section, then the bitch owner is not entitled to a free repeat stud; however, most stud dog owners would be sympathetic and allow a free return to the stud dog. In many cases if the bitch has to be neutered because of problems at whelping, a stud owner will allow the free return to another bitch belonging to the bitch owner.

It must be made clear that the bitch and the dog are healthy, in good condition, and not suffering from any infectious disease at the time of mating. Some stud owners require that the bitch be swabbed to make sure she is not carrying infection of the uterus, which could affect the stud dog, making him sterile.

All this seems like a minefield, but if everything is written down and signed by both parties, in the main everything works out well.

SIRE IDENTITY

In the twenty-first century we are more aware of permanently identifying dogs, and this is useful for a number of reasons. If a stud dog is not the only dog that mated a bitch on that season, DNA can determine which of the two is the sire of the puppies. It would not be considered ethical to mate a bitch to two different dogs in the same season intentionally, but it could occur by accident, for instance if a dog managed to get into the bitch's home environment, or if a male she lived with mated her before you realized that she had started her season. It may even be that she is caught by a dog puppy you thought wasn't old enough to know about mating bitches.

WHEN TO USE A DOG AT STUD

Small breeds often reach maturity earlier than large breeds, which is why it is more acceptable to breed from bitches from around eighteen months in toy breeds of dog, yet it is considered undesirable to mate a bitch in larger breeds until they are two years or over. The same applies to the age a dog is ready to be used at stud – though of course there is always the exception to the rule, and a lot depends on the mental maturity of the dog. Other factors also influence his ability to 'work'.

Breeders often think it a good idea to use a dog at stud whilst he is quite young, even before he is a year old, as he will then refrain from mating bitches until he is around eighteen months of age. The theory behind this, is that the dog that is used young retains what to do – though he should not be over-used whilst he is so young, so that he can grow on and develop.

I once heard of a dog 'catching a bitch' when the owner's husband let them out together: the male was only five months old! The husband was severely reprimanded, but the bitch was not given a misalliance injection, as the dog was considered to be too young. However, the bitch had ten puppies!

A young dog may be brought to an in-season bitch with a view to him mating her, and he just plays, showing no recognition that the bitch is in season. If this is the case, treat it as a game, just tell him how good he is, and remove him from the area.

On no account attempt to force him, as this could put him off for life. Patience will bring its own virtues.

As a dog becomes older he may find it difficult to mount a bitch; hopefully you will realize when the time has come to withdraw your dog from stud work. People can be very insistent in trying to persuade you to let them use him 'this one last time'. They will extol his virtues, and claim that this is the bitch they have bred just to go with your boy: his puppies are turning out so well and he has produced such quality, no other dog is in the running. He has the 'old lines', which we so need to retain.

All this is good for your ego, to hear such wonderful eulogies on your beloved dog. But look, he is probably ten years or over at this time, so these people have actually had at least nine years in which to use him.

Show your dog the respect he deserves, and if he is having difficulty mating bitches, then decline these people their request.

There is a peculiar anomaly amongst many 'dog folk', that as soon as a dog is withdrawn from stud he becomes the only dog to use. Possibly it is a form of

An older dog, who now only dreams of his past as top stud dog!

one-upmanship, the 'I used him, but no one else can' syndrome. There is also the dog you were once in competition against, but which has long been retired and as such is not a rival, that suddenly appeals as a stud. Or as a dog becomes unavailable, its faults suddenly vanish in a rosy hue over the mists of time.

We humans can be strange creatures.

PREPARING THE STUD DOG

Preparing the dog mentally for stud work might sound a little far-fetched, but when the breeder orchestrates a coupling between two dogs, the procedure is taking away natural selection. Natural selection, it has to be said, is not always the ideal, and over centuries 'breeders' of animals and plants have devised the breeding of their fancy to the betterment of the species.

Remembering that you are the leader of the pack, and the dog will look to you, his leader, for confidence and approval. Dogs are very aware of what you are thinking and feeling, so if you are a little apprehensive, even nervous, as many inexperienced stud dog owners are, this anxiety will be passed to the dog faster than jungle drums. For those who are innocent in the art of mating dogs, any anxiety they feel derives from the abnormal experience of physically wanting the dogs to copulate with them watching – almost taking part, to be bluntly honest.

Having grown up in a farming environment, animals copulating was a normal process for the benefit of evolution, as far as I was concerned. This is how an experienced dog breeder, and particularly a stud dog owner, would see it, which makes the procedure quite normal, and therefore encouraging for the young dog. The ideal scenario for mating a dog for its first time would be to have an experienced handler in charge of the proceedings. Of course this is not always practical, but it can make the difference between having a proficient stud dog or a tricky one.

The good stud dog starts when he is a baby, probably as early as twelve weeks of age. Surprised? Remember the puppy that gets over-excited and starts humping a cushion or someone's leg? Owner is embarrassed, so instantly rushes to pull him away. Puppy thinks, wow, that's a good way to get immediate attention, must try that again. What's more, he is not humping as a sexual act, but it happens when he is over-excited and it 'feels rather nice'.

The correct way to handle this situation is as follows: when puppy is starting to become a little too animated, casually go to him with a toy chew that he enjoys, and talk soothingly and stroke his head whilst giving him the distracting plaything. This dissolves the situation. Scolding a young dog will only make him nervous of your approach.

Be aware that dogs that hump everything and anything don't make good stud dogs, as they don't know, or ever have, an end result of their actions.

As a young dog gains in age and self-assurance, probably from around six months of age, he will possibly start thinking more about sex when playing with a bitch that may be coming into season, or has just finished her season. But even though he will sniff around her and dash about like the Cock of the North, underneath he will probably be quite apprehensive, and could easily be put off. (*See* Chapter 6, Mating.)

Playing with a bitch in season will excite the male to perform.

THE ANATOMY OF THE MALE DOG

It is generally considered that a male canine reaches sexual maturity at between six and eight months of age. Smaller breeds are more likely to be earlier than large breeds, although this is not binding. The male is able and often very willing to copulate at any time. He is fertile (unless he has problems) from this young age, right up until he is unable to mount a bitch, in all probability because of advancing age. This is unlike the female, which is only able to reproduce when she is in season and ovulating, normally every six months.

Dogs are more interested in procreation as the nights start to become lighter and the climate becomes more clement. This could be a throwback to their ancestors, who mated in the spring, probably because with the rise in temperature, the offspring had a better chance of survival.

The reproductive organs of the dog are not as important to the breeder as those of the bitch, because he supplies the sperm but does not have any effect on how puppies are delivered. However, it is useful to know how everything works, as this will help an understanding of stud work, and why problems may arise.

The normal reproductive tract of the male genital organs includes the following: the urethra and penis (enclosed by a sheath), the passages through which urine and sperm are passed; the epididymis; the deferens duct, the tube that leads from the epididymis to the urethra; two testicles, encased within the scrotum; the spermatic cord; and the prostate gland.

The testicles or testes: These are oval in shape and tend to be thicker in the middle than from side to side, with one slightly behind the other. If the testes are one directly in front of the other, there could be a penchant for genetic crypt-

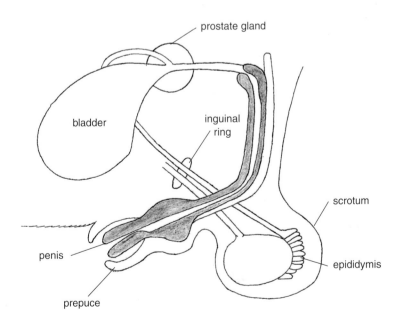

The reproductive tract of the male dog.

prostate gland

bladder

inguinal ring

scrotum

penis

epididymis

prepuce

CARE OF THE STUD DOG

To be successful and reliable the stud dog must be in optimum health. So he should be fed a quality diet, good husbandry also plays a vital part, and he should be exercised according to his physical and mental needs.

It is thought that if a stud dog is not used for a period of time, the sperm may not be in prime condition; however, we have never found this to be the case. A dog used for the first time can and often does produce quality sperm to fertilize the eggs, producing a normal or even large litter. Likewise we have never found that a dog that has not been used for a time falls short in its capability to produce puppies.

A dog should be kept in prime health; a quality food is essential to his wellbeing.

orchism to crop up. However, this positioning could also happen if the dog has particularly well-defined muscles in his quarters.

The testes perform the task of producing sperm and testosterone, the male hormone. They are held in the scrotum, a thin hairless sack or pouch, because this is the ideal way to keep the temperature tolerable. They need to be several degrees lower in temperature than that of the abdomen in order to keep the sperm functioning normally. In cold weather the scrotum contracts to protect the testes, and it often expands in hot weather, again in order to keep the testes, and therefore also the sperm, at a constant temperature.

The scrotum is divided by a thin wall, which separates the testes, each of which is connected to an epididymis.

The epididymis: A large tube, its head and tail positioned at the front and back of each testicle. A different duct, the ductus deferens, starts at the tail of the epididymis and runs along the border of the testicle into the abdominal cavity through the inguinal canal. It passes through the prostate and empties into the urethra.

The spermatic cords: Are composed of the ductus deferens, plus the blood vessels and nerve supply to the testicles. These cords also originate at the tail of the epididymis and extend through the inguinal canal.

The prostate gland: Surrounds the neck of the bladder, just below the rectum. When it becomes inflamed it can show a swelling under the tail, and blood appears in the urine. This usually means that ultimately the dog will have to be castrated and the prostate gland removed. The vet can sometimes control the condition. In an older dog castration is more probably the case.

The penis: An extremely vascular structure, containing vessels and connective tissue, which is specialized to produce an erection; this facilitates penetration of the penis into the vagina. It is composed of a number of parts: the root, body and the glans penis. The root and body are constructed of squishy tissue and a bone. The glans penis is the soft portion of the penis: breeders often refer to this part as the 'bulbs'. During copulation, the glans penis swells, appearing as two bulbs at the root of the engorged penis, locking the penis into the vagina of the bitch.

The moist protective covering of the non-erect penis is the prepuce and is capable of secreting smegma, a thick lubricating liquid.

FERTILITY

A normal male constantly produces sperm from puberty, though it declines in later years, unlike a female which is born with all the eggs she will ever have to ovulate.

As large breeds generally age faster than smaller breeds, there is more chance of age-related fertility problems sooner, in large breeds. As a general rule, the larger breeds are at their most fertile between the ages of two to about six years of age. In small breeds and toys the fertility span is greater, between around two years to seven or eight years of age.

If a stud dog is missing getting bitches in whelp – perhaps three bitches, one after another, have not produced puppies when mated to that particular stud dog – it may be worth taking him to the vet and having his sperm tested. The reason you would wait until after he has mated three bitches is that the problem could be with a bitch, or a bitch may not be ovulating when mated; however, three in succession is one too many to be a coincidence. Taking him to the vet could help to find potential disease early, when there are no other untoward signs.

INFERTILITY

If a stud dog achieves less than 75 per cent pregnancy in bitches of known fertility, and is himself in obviously good health, outwardly at least, it is worth having his fertility evaluated via a test collection at the vet. Your normal practitioner may refer you to a vet who specializes in canine fertility, as results can be affected by the way the sample is collected, either because the dog is stressed by an inexperienced handler or if urine is allowed into the sample. Urine can kill sperm, which is probably why when a dog is asked to mate a bitch, he will often sniff her and go off to cock his leg a number of times before climbing on the bitch to mate.

Most dogs ejaculate in three parts. The initial fluid is clear to slightly cloudy; this is before the release of the sperm. The second part is milky white and thick, as this is rich with sperm; and this is followed by the last part, from the prostate, which should be a clear liquid. Any blood or urine in the sample will affect the result. Each part is analysed separately, and if an infection is evident in any part, identification will be found during analysis; this is why it is better to have a specialist in the field of fertility taking the sample and analysing it.

If blood is found in the third part the vet will be able to treat the dog for prostate problems immediately. To obtain a sample a teaser bitch in season, preferably at peak oestrus is needed, as this will heighten his desire, which will account for a better sample.

Infection of the Testes

Infection will almost certainly manifest itself by swelling, pain and inflammation of the testicles and/or scrotum.

With chronic inflammation, the affected tissue will probably be quite hard; the surrounding tissue will be soft, as it will start to deteriorate. Infection will raise the temperature in the area, damaging the sperm. If caught early enough antibiotic treatment should solve the condition, the dog resuming normal production of sperm. In extreme cases the dog may need at least one testicle removed; if one can be saved it should still be able to produce healthy sperm.

Cryptorchism and Monorchism

If a dog's testicles fail to descend into the scrotum he is monorchid and invariably sterile. If one only is descended, he is classed as cryptorchid. In this instance he would probably be able to sire puppies but as this condition is often hereditary it is advisable not to use a dog at stud with this complaint.

Retained testicles are therefore stuck in an atmosphere where the temperature is too hot for them; abnormalities often occur, leading to possible cancer, usually in later life. Of course this leads to an operation, which is always more of a risk in an older dog. For this reason it is wise to effect castration early in the dog's life, preferably before he reaches sexual maturity, leading to him having a more relaxed mental state. He can lead his life without feeling the need to be dominant, and he won't have the desire to look for bitches in season.

If the dog receives an injury to the scrotum this could result in damage to the reproductive tract; this in turn could reduce sperm health, and could also affect his ability to mate bitches. Injury to the penis will have the same effects.

Tumours

Tumors could occur in the testes, which would involve removal of the affected testicle. The dog could still be used at stud, but it may be in his best interest to be castrated. Environmental issues can cause problems with fertility. Toxins and chemicals used on the land the dog is exercised on, and blowing in the atmosphere, could cause problems.

Thyroid Problems

Thyroid problems can arise in males, which can influence fertility, lowering the production and quality of sperm and decreasing the size of the testicles. Dogs with a low or decreased libido may be unable to produce the hormone testosterone, or it may not reach the brain. A dog's mental confidence will affect his ability to 'work', as will stress levels.

ARTIFICIAL INSEMINATION

Artificial insemination (AI) can be beneficial to dog breeders because it widens the gene pool in numerically small breeds, or when outcrosses are required to develop lines that are in danger of becoming too introvert. However, it is not a good idea to contemplate this form of breeding if you find that a stud dog won't 'work' or a bitch is aggressive and therefore cannot be mated naturally. Why would you want to reproduce animals that have character defects?

There is also the possibility that you want to use a dog that died years before. That's fine, as long as you remember that the perfect dog has not yet been born, and his negatives must be evaluated along with his attributes. Too often we commit to memory only the good things about a dog we once knew, now that he is no longer in competition against our stock. You must be realistic if you are breeding for the future of the breed.

It can be exciting, however, to bring in new blood from abroad, it may be cheaper to actually bring the dog rather than the semen. The process of AI is time-consuming and expensive, and does not always provide the required results.

Before you start, you must carry out research to find a vet who specializes in canine reproduction and AI. Although this practice has been carried out in cattle and other species for many decades, it is comparatively new in canines and requires an experienced vet, who not only performs the insemination, but can also evaluate the sperm and gauge likely success rates.

The bitch will need to be swabbed or blood tested at regular intervals by the vet to determine the level of the hormone progesterone, denoting oestrus. Trust your vet. We had a litter by AI. We took the bitch every other day to the vet for testing, and the vet administered the AI on the bitch's fifteenth day in season; I naively thought this quite late, but relied on the vet's experience. The bitch delivered nine healthy puppies.

We were fortunate that we had an excellent vet qualified in this field locally – which is another thing to consider when thinking about the use of artificial insemination.

The vet will impregnate the bitch either by transcervical/endoscopy or by the vaginal method. The Royal College of Veterinary Surgeons feels that surgical inseminations can have disadvantages so this is only allowed by the KC in exceptional circumstances. Consent must be sought before using this method or registration of puppies could be denied.

The Kennel Club has an information guide on regulations relating to the requirement of using artificial insemination, and should be consulted before embarking on the process, as rules and regulations can change. It would be extremely depressing to have organized everything to past specifications, only to find they had been amended.

At present the Kennel Club will, as a general rule, only accept registration of puppies from the Irish Wolfhound breed which are the progeny of a bitch that has been inseminated by a donor sire which is

---

IMPORTED SEMEN

If you wish to import semen, the following are some points to think about:

- Make sure you see the dog, or at least his progeny, in the flesh, and not just his pedigree. Hearsay can lose faults and gain virtues!
- Permanent identification is essential; DNA is the most efficient method of both sire and semen identification. Health tests should have been achieved on the donor of the semen, and copies of these results available to you.
- Make sure your preparations are accurate, and keep copies of all relative documentation, just in case of problems.
- Contact the KC and the ministry for animal health and welfare (DEFRA); you will need permission for the registration of puppies (KC), and a licence for the importation of semen (DEFRA).
- Semen can either be frozen, as explained above, or chilled. Chilled semen should be used within twenty-four hours.

alive and resident in this country, and if the said sire is over eight and a half years old. This is because the gene pool for this breed is small, and dogs over this age will possibly have trouble mating a bitch in the conventional manner.

Other requests which are made to the Kennel Club would be the need for new blood lines, or to widen the gene pool as the breed is in decline, or to reintroduce old lines. It could be that the chosen stud has been exported, and no suitable stud is available in this country. The breeder may have semen stored from a dog before he died, and this will help to re-establish their line. Semen can be collected, frozen in liquid nitrogen canisters, and kept for many years.

For reasons that will improve the health, conformation, temperament and type of a breed, the KC will give AI due consideration.

Obtaining Semen

To obtain semen you will obviously need the stud dog, also a 'teaser bitch', which must be in season, preferably in oestrus.

To obtain optimum semen the stud dog should be worry free, so a confident handler and experienced vet are necessary to put him at his ease.

As he is excited by the bitch and mounts her, his penis is directed into an artificial vagina and stimulated to affect ejaculation. The collected sperm cells are examined on a slide by the vet to ensure that they are sufficiently concentrated, mobile and anatomically normal. It is essential that the sperm is strong, active, normal and plentiful; otherwise they will not freeze adequately to fertilize the eggs. It is not always possible to determine if the sperm are totally healthy, as there may be flaws way down in the molecular level of the DNA in the sperm that is making the dog sterile. So AI is not an easy or a cheap option, and studies have found that there is only a 65 to 85 per cent success rate; but used truthfully it can be a useful tool in improving the health and overall quality of purebred canines, helping to eliminate undesirable genetic characteristics, and expanding gene pools.

6 MATING

THE BITCH

It has been established that a bitch must be over one year old and under eight years old when she is mated, and should not be allowed to have another litter of puppies within one year of a previous litter if the puppies are to be registered with the governing body – the Kennel Club. There may be extenuating circumstances when the KC will allow the registration of puppies from a bitch at the edge of these limits. However, application to the KC must be made prior to mating, explaining any valid reason for the exception, and if this is not observed you may find you have a litter of puppies that you are unable to register, meaning that you will not be eligible to compete in Kennel Club licensed events.

DETECTING OVULATION

It is a good idea to watch the bitch throughout any seasons she may have prior to the one when she is intended to be mated, in particular recording when she goes out of colour (when the blood gives way to a clear discharge, generally indicating that she is in oestrus). It should also be noted when she 'stands', as this is an indication of oestrus for future reference. This is much easier to identify when a bitch lives with other dogs. Whilst they

Flirting is necessary for each to become aroused.

will play as normal, as the excitement of the game intensifies, she will stand, arch her back and turn her tail for the others to ride her, stimulating copulation; this is the signal that she is getting ready to be mated.

If no pre-mate tests are to be done, the best suggestion is that she is likely to be ovulating two to three days after she displays this behaviour. This allows you time to contact the stud dog owner to say you will be over in two days' time – there is no need to call the stud owner in a panic and rush over straightaway. (You will, of course, have pre-booked the stud after careful thought on your choice, as previously explained.)

If your bitch is the only dog you have and you are inexperienced in the mating procedure, it will not be so easy. Count the start of her season when she first drops blood; this is generally noticeable if you are vigilant. A bitch usually goes out of colour at around the eleventh day of her season, when she is starting to come into oestrus; however, some bitches may bleed throughout their season, so don't just go with this assumption alone. A couple of weeks before she commences her season, you may observe a change in her personality: she could become a little depressed, and as time progresses her vulva will noticeably swell. When she is taken for a walk, male dogs may start to show a strong interest in her.

If you are using a stud dog that knows his job and whose owners have expertise in breeding and mating, they should sympathize with your lack of experience and may suggest that you bring your bitch over at around her tenth or eleventh day in season, just to see how she reacts in the presence of a male. If possible you will already have met up with owner and stud dog, and they, if

knowledgeable, will have given you some tips on what to look for, so you can identify when your bitch is ready for mating.

It is probably not wise to use a novice dog. In this scenario, the two beginner owners tend to let the dogs get on with it, so the two dash around the garden, flirting and pouncing at each other, and this goes on for half an hour, or longer. The dog could start to mount the bitch, she swings around. Eventually they become exhausted. They sense your apprehension, which affects their confidence and mood. If left together at this stage the dog will be so tired and hesitant that he will not look forward to approaching a bitch in season, and this could spoil him for future studwork.

So if both parties are inexperienced, enrol the help of a person proficient in studwork, to give the dog confidence. They will know if he is ready mentally to mate a bitch. Don't just expect this person to help at a moment's notice: you will have to make contact with them beforehand, inform them of likely dates and organize a time to meet. You may have to pay a handling fee.

THE MATING PROCEDURE

As the mating procedure becomes more intense, the bitch will become more receptive to the male, twitching her vulva as he licks her, and her tail will move dramatically to one side as she pushes her rump up to the dog. He will mount her and his body will pump faster towards her as he becomes more aroused. His penis will come out of the sheath, and move faster towards her vulva. It is wise to have an experienced person to hand at this time to step in, if necessary, to restrain the bitch and stop her snapping,

The tie, the male and female are locked together.

as the maiden bitch (a bitch who has not been mated before) may twist and shriek as the dog enters her. This is more out of shock than anything else. Canines do not have a hymen, so she does not need 'breaking in'. If she genuinely cannot be entered, the vet should be consulted. During foreplay he will emit fluid, which will lubricate her. If really necessary, because he cannot enter her, Vaseline can be applied to the vulva.

If the bitch is not a maiden she will probably stand hard, accepting the dog, knowing what is to come. Even a maiden that was mated two days previously and has returned 'just to make sure' for a second mating, will often stand perfectly still on the second mating.

The Young Dog
A young dog of about four and a half to five months will take an interest in a bitch in season, and will possibly flirt with her and mount her, though it is unlikely that he is capable of actually mating with her – however the operative word is 'unlikely'.

So whilst he should not be scolded, you must be careful that he is not allowed to follow through his actions.

So in these circumstances approach the youngster with a playful attitude, perhaps with a toy to distract him. This takes his attention from the bitch because he is curious as to what you are doing. You can guide him away from the bitch with the toy, and remove him from the area altogether. Obviously have that little game with him so he is happy with the result. If he is too intent on the bitch, pat him and gently remove him from the bitch, all the time praising him. Once again, do something which makes him happy to go with you, because this way he takes confidence from your support of his actions. All too often, when asked to help with a difficult mating, I find that the dog will have uncertainties about mating the bitch. He will play around like Mr Super Stud, but when it comes to mounting the bitch he looks to his owner and loses any confidence he had. This implies to me that a raised, cross voice

This young Pharaoh Hound is showing potential even at this young age.

has been used whenever the youngster has 'tried it on' with a bitch.

It is a natural reaction to speak with a sharp tone to a young dog when you think he is going to mate a bitch in error. Instinctively you just want him to stop immediately, so that the accidental mating is aborted. It may even be the case that you are vexed with him fussing round the in-season bitch, and your reaction is out of frustration. However, it is actually your fault that he is put in this position, since Nature and the evolution of the species condone that he behaves in this manner.

It must be understood that it is extremely unkind to keep an entire male and a female in season in proximity. Even one in a kennel outside and the other inside the house is quite often too close. So if you own entire canines of the opposite sex, be sure that when the bitch comes into season, one of the animals is removed to a boarding kennels or a friend's house for three weeks.

If your breeding establishment is purpose-built, you will have organized things so that you have adequate facilities for any in-season bitches to be housed completely away from any other dogs, thus keeping the male relaxed, as he will not see a bitch or even know they are in season. If he is kept away from a bitch but near enough to smell that she is in season, his instinct will be that he wants to get to her, to mate her, and in this instance he will become agitated and stressed, probably lose weight, and become very vocal in his quest to get at her.

If you have ever had a bitch in season and taken her for a walk, you will probably be only too aware that you will have stray dogs howling on your doorstep in the middle of the night!

The young dog will sometimes play with a toy or blanket, becoming sexually excited and humping the object of his attention as the game progresses. This can lead to him 'tying' outside his body, which at first sight is quite alarming. The penis grows large and becomes very red as it is engorged with blood, and the bulbs at the base of the penis are swollen; if this happens, there is nothing that can be done until the tie naturally subsides, when everything will revert to normal. I recall the owner of a dog we had bred ringing us in a distressed state to say that it had 'turned himself inside out'. I was at a loss to know what she meant, until she explained. I could then reassure her!

Of course, many people have related the story of the terrier that humps people's legs, usually guests or children. Terriers are quick, active dogs by nature; they are bred to dispose of fast-moving vermin, so they can be easily excited. This can lead to sexual excitement, which is when a terrier might hump the leg! He does not necessarily realize that this is a sexual feeling that happens on instinct, it is just that it feels good! When young, dogs don't have the control of their feelings, which comes with maturity (rather like humans!). So the terrier, and other breeds with this sort of character, will play with children, who often don't see the signs of over-enthusiastic behaviour, therefore the dog starts to hump the child, as he would with his littermates.

The adult instantly reprimands the dog, so the dog will not want to perform this action when adults are around, which is why he chooses young members of the family and unconnected adults who are unlikely to tell him off. It also gives him a feeling of dominance – and it gets him instant attention, because you rush to stop him. So if he is bored and requiring interaction, he knows this habit will instantly make you take notice of him.

As male dogs reach puberty they can become very full of themselves and think they know everything. This is when you,

the pack leader, must reaffirm his lower position in the pecking order. Adolescence might show itself in different forms according to the variety. In small breeds the dog will perhaps start to cock his leg at various places within the home, even though he has been house-trained for a considerable time. This is an irritating habit, which can be difficult to stop.

If he is a large breed – and this principally occurs amongst breeds with dominant tendencies – he might stand up to you, questioning your supremacy as pack leader. This situation must be dealt with carefully. Bullying him will make him lose confidence in you and will reduce any chance of him being a successful stud. Your control should be stated with confidence, but compassionately. I can relate a classic example: we have always kept our large breed of dogs as a pack, only removing bitches when they come into season. Watching the pack, I noticed that a fit dog of four years old, and therefore in his prime, was lying in the field just chewing a bone. A nine-year-old male, obviously not as strong or fit as the younger, wandered up and stood over this vigorous male. This chap, being in a vulnerable position, gave up his bone to the old dog, which walked away and subsequently discarded it. The moral here was that the old dog confirmed his supremacy without confrontation.

It is important to apply these rules. We can go to the level of the dog, but he should not come up to our rank. Faced with a situation of 'stand-off', it is difficult to suppress vexation, so think before you act. Don't rush in or he will automatically be on the defensive, which is bite first, ask questions later.

Try to attract his interest by doing something that he enjoys. Assuming you are successful, think about going back to basics in future. If he was on furniture, which is not allowed, put a chair on the sofa so he can't get on it. You made the rule he couldn't disobey, and the point was made with no confrontation. A good way to display who is boss, is always go through a door or gate first, and if he tries to push past, block his way and stand quietly until he settles, and only proceed when he allows you to proceed first. Physiologically you will earn his respect, and being top of the pack he will be confident in you when it comes to mating bitches.

Mating Quarters

It is prudent to have separate mating quarters, away from prying eyes and the noise of the other dogs, so the dog can concentrate on the job in hand. He will, over time, know that when he goes to this area he has been brought there for mating, so this mentally prepares him. It is useful if this area can have outside and indoor facilities, to cater for all weather conditions, and which are contained so the dogs cannot escape, giving them the freedom to become acclimatized to each other. Avoid areas that contain anything that could cause harm to the dogs if they are dashing about; also check that there are no small crevices where one of the dogs could try to hide and become trapped.

When he is presented with his first bitch in season – and even better if she is not a maiden – protect him from the viewing public. It is amazing how people want to bring friends and children (maybe they feel it is good for sex education!); however, politely ask that everyone other than the handlers waits inside. Once the tie is effected they can pop out and quietly watch at this time.

Initially the bitch should be allowed to relieve herself and get her bearings; she may have had a long journey, and has arrived at a strange place. Following this,

Hold the bitch firmly, or muzzle her. The male must have confidence that he will never be allowed to be bitten.

take her to the mating quarters. When the dog is brought in, be aware that she may snap at him, so tread carefully, and oversee their initial meeting in order to gauge her reactions. It is wise to have a slip lead available and a muzzle in your pocket every time you prepare to mate dogs, because even the most genial bitch can act out of character when she is being mated, particularly if you are using an experienced dog that is not too bothered by foreplay. Muzzled, she cannot bite either dog or handler out of alarm or fear – and once bitten, your potential stud dog could end up never wanting to mate a bitch again. So don't take the risk. Obviously the bitch can still object verbally, but if the stud dog has never been snapped at or bitten, he will be supremely confident in his handler and will mate the bitch despite her objection.

As the owner of a competent stud dog, this makes for an easier life. Furthermore, if you have owners coming from miles away with a bitch, it makes for a more congenial operation if they know that both you and the stud dog are gentle but confident.

The lead can control her and remove her quickly if she is going to bite the dog. If this is the case, remove one or other of the pair, whilst the muzzle is securely attached to her. If you try to do this in the mating quarters and hold the dog back it just leads to confusion all round and possible injury.

Some people are of the conviction that if a bitch objects, she should not be mated. I respect this opinion, but feel that many different breeds react differently. Weimaraners are a positive-thinking, quick-acting breed, and a bitch will flirt and stand turning her tail, all signs that she is desperate to be mated, yet when the dog mounts her, she will spin round

and snap at him menacingly. Once tied, she is sweetness itself. Yet again, many setters will stand rock solid as the tie is achieved, then the bitch will swing round and squiggle and squirm. This is another very good reason for having a knowledgeable, experienced handler present.

Overseeing the Mating
So the pair have been introduced; the dog will probably start by trotting around, ears up and high-stepping, then will sniff and lick the bitch's genitals. If she is absolutely ready, her vulva will probably twitch and she will raise up her hindquarters.

As time goes on, he will wander around and cock his leg a lot, which is a sign that he is preparing to mate her. The reason he cocks his leg so much is to empty his bladder, because urine can kill sperm and could be emitted at the time of ejaculation.

Mating Small Breeds
With small breeds, the two are often allowed to play so they can get to know each other, and to encourage the dog to think about mating. As he starts to get excited and to mount her, the two will be lifted on to a firm table equipped with a non-slip rubber mat, or often a grooming trolley, as the surface of this is perfect; like this it is easier to help with the proceedings, and to hold the bitch still. Often patting the bitch with the palm of your hand flat on her back encourages the dog to mount her.

If he is insecure about climbing on the bitch, encourage him all the time with a soft voice, and lift the bitch up bodily: doing this makes him think she is being removed, so he will often climb on and grab her with his forelegs round her loin and flanks. Let him try a few times, so as

These Pugs are 'tied' and naturally stand back to back, as a defence tactic.

to get the testosterone levels flowing. He will thrust, affecting the penis towards the vagina. When a dog mates, his penis does not go hard and swell until he has entered the bitch, unlike other males, so the penile bone is the part that takes the penis into the vagina.

If he is not getting near enough, put your first finger and thumb on each side of the vulva from underneath, and guide the vulva towards his penis. As the penis enters the vulva, with your other hand gently push him forwards: your fingers around the vulva allows you to feel that his penis is entirely in, so that as his bulbs swell he will be held in behind the bitch's sphincter muscle.

It is important that you avoid touching his penis, as this will make him think that he has entered the bitch and the penis will swell, making it impossible for him to enter her: he will effectively have tied outside the bitch. If this happens, he will ejaculate and the penis will remain swollen for a considerable time. It is unlikely that a young, inexperienced dog will be able to mate again that day. Stay with him, gently reassure him that all is well, but don't pester him. He will probably be bemused or a little worried by the effect of his action, but let him sort himself out.

When he has successfully tied inside the bitch, the handlers need to keep a firm but gentle hold on both dog and bitch. Some bitches start to jostle about, which could hurt and alarm the dog; moreover, they could both topple off the table. If the bitch does react in this way, let them settle for a minute, then either let the dog, or you, lift his front legs off her. He may then want to turn back to back with the bitch, and you can assist if needs be.

Mating Large Breeds

Mating large breeds can need a little more strength from the handlers. Restraining the bitch must be firm but not threatening: remember she is in a strange environment with a dog she is unacquainted with pursuing her, and an unfamiliar handler in close proximity. Their foreplay could get rougher than it would with smaller breeds, so be careful: as they dash about they won't be concentrating on anything except the performance in hand, and could bang into you.

If a young dog is playing but does not climb on the bitch, lifting up her front legs can often encourage him. If this fails to arouse him, carefully lift her up bodily and turn her round – this usually has the desired effect. Let him gain confidence by climbing on her a few times before you intervene. If half an hour or more passes and he is showing no interest in mating her, perhaps he is mentally immature. Don't sour him, but put him away and use another dog, even if the bitch has to be taken to a dog from a different kennel altogether.

If things go according to plan and he then climbs on the bitch and starts thrusting, he may need the guidance of you holding the vulva (as explained above, as for smaller breeds); in bigger breeds, it is best to put your hand through the bitch's hind legs from the flank area, because that way you can control her if she starts to sit down. Try to avert your face from staring at the male at this point: it must be off-putting to be mating a bitch with someone on your

level looking straight at you. His thrusting will increase as he enters the bitch, at which point put your leg or your free hand behind him to make sure he does not fall backwards and slip out of the bitch before his bulbs swell. With a young dog, his enthusiasm and inexperience could lead him to being excessively zealous and trying to climb too high on the back of the bitch, lifting his back legs off the ground, and as a result he will overbalance.

If the breed being mated is long coated it can be a good idea to remove some of the hair around her rear, or at least move it well away from the area of her vulva. Hair can be taken inside the bitch by the penis, and can then get caught around the penis or even attach into it, which could cause an infection or at the very least a lot of pain.

The Tie

Immediately after the tie the bitch may squeak and struggle; a maiden bitch could show alarm, so hold her firmly around the body and soothe her. The tighter you hold her head, the more she will struggle to be free. Holding her head tightly will make her become claustrophobic. Of course if she is wiggling about and trying to be free she must be restrained, in which case it is far better to hold her body around the area of her flanks and loin; this will still allow her forequarters to move around, but will prevent her from pulling the dog about. She will almost certainly settle after a moment or two. At this time the muzzle, if used, can be removed, unless the breed has idiosyncrasies, in which case it would be advisable that she remain muzzled.

When dogs are tied it is perfectly natural for them to 'turn': either the male will drop his forelegs to the floor at one side

Holding dogs that are tied stops them trying to pull apart and prevents potential damage to either.

of the bitch, and may stay in this position for the length of the tie; or he will lift one back leg to follow the forelegs, consequently ending up back-to-back with the bitch. Although this might appear to be a painful way of placing themselves, the dogs are not uncomfortable – though why they tie like this is a matter of much thought.

My interpretation is this: because dogs are pack animals that live with other males in the group, a pecking order must exist for the equilibrium of the pack – therefore the alpha male is the one who fathers the offspring. If he mated a bitch and immediately dismounted, another lesser male could mate her, and because canines are multi-egg producing, this would mean that the alpha male would be responsible for another's offspring. The fact that they are locked together for a relatively long time gives the sperm time to reach the eggs, which are there-fore fertilized before another male has a chance to mate her.

Another thought is that the tie gives enough time for the three phases of ejac-ulate to be dispensed. This is logical in one sense, but since nature is so clever, why not a more rapid ejaculate, as in other animals?

The reason that the pair turns back to back might have evolved again as a result of the pack situation: tied in this way both dog and bitch have mobile forequarters and the ability to use head and teeth, so they can protect themselves from other pack members who might come too close and become too interested.

The tie may last for only a few minutes, or it might last for an hour or more – I have heard of a tie lasting one and a half hours! It is usually about twenty minutes, however, and when tied, there is no way of parting dog and bitch – even buckets of cold water will not effect a release!

Once the initial shock of the tie has subsided, you will probably find the pair are as bored as you are, standing about. As you are holding the dogs chatting, you may find yourselves moving round the area quite a lot, and this is normal. The dogs don't have to stay in the same place, in fact if you try to make them be perfectly still, they will become more agitated and may try to pull away from you. The reason you are holding them is for mental support, and to make sure neither tries to pull away sharply, which could hurt either one of them.

Obviously dogs mate and stand around with no one to hold them to no ill effect, as seen on street corners. This is not suggested practice, however, because responsible mating of dogs will prevent them from trying to pull apart, when they could cause damage to either party. If the dog is injured he is likely to recall the pain when asked to mate a bitch again, and this will make him insecure. This would not make for a confident stud dog.

It can happen that the pair part while the penis is still engorged with blood. It is a rare occurrence, but we did once experience this with a skilled stud dog. We bathed the penis with clean cold water to no avail, and ultimately we had to go to the vet and have him sedated to allow release. Thankfully this didn't happen again, and he went on to mate bitches successfully.

The pair don't actually need to tie in order to produce puppies, as is proved with AI. I have also known a bitch which was mated, and when the dog was fully inside her, he was allowed to turn – only to find he came out, fully tied. This was repeated with the same result, nevertheless the bitch duly whelped a healthy litter of seven puppies.

HOW MANY ATTEMPTS ARE NEEDED?

One mating on the correct day when the bitch is in oestrus between a healthy fertile pair should produce puppies. Many people prefer two matings, however. This is really as 'insurance', in case the bitch was a little early in oestrus and the eggs were not ready. Sometimes both parties agree on a third mating, but this is not really required if the pair tied properly on the previous occasions, perhaps only if there had been a 'slip' mating

DNA TESTING

As previously stated, DNA testing is a positive way of permanently identifying a canine. It would be useful if a bitch had been suspected of being miss-mated, as the puppies could be DNA-tested for paternity. This form of identification is very easy and painless to execute. You apply to the KC for a kit, on a request form from the KC. The form will have the registration details of the dog, its name, registration number, breed, date of birth, sire and dam's names and registration numbers, plus the owner's details and of course the fee. You will be sent a tube with the dog's details on, containing a swab. The swab is removed and rubbed gently inside the dog's cheek, as instructed. This is air dried, avoiding contamination, sealed and returned by post to the laboratory, where it is checked to reveal the unique DNA of that dog. Not only is this used for identification, but it is useful in determining genetic disorders.

The Kennel Club charitable trust has provided substantial funds to facilitate developing further DNA testing schemes for diseases that are known to affect certain breeds, which is commendable and can only add to improving the future health of dogs.

(when the dog ties inside the bitch, but the bulbs are not in far enough for the bitch to hold him in the tie, and he slips out). However, a slip mating can still produce puppies, so don't be tempted to mate the bitch with another dog.

So as long as multiple matings are acceptable to both parties, this is absolutely fine. There is little point in mating on consecutive days, since sperm and eggs will still be viable on the second day; the general rule is to mate, leave a day in between, and mate again. If the bitch is not quite in oestrus, it is better to give two days for insurance.

The eggs remain capable of being fertilized for two days during oestrus, before any deterioration may be ex-pected after maturation, with the added advantage that sperm is able to survive for four or five days in the uterus. In young fit animals the periphery could easily be increased.

For these reasons you must be careful to keep the bitch away from any other male, as rare though it may be, there is the possibility that she could conceive to different males. If this accidental mating of more than one male did take place, the KC must be informed and both dogs' details submitted with the registration of the litter.

On Completion of Mating
As the pair prepares to cease the tie, they will want to lick around the genital area.

This bitch is enjoying resting in the back of the car on completion of mating, whilst the paperwork is concluded.

They will have been 'locked' together for a long period of time and should have settled calmly; this will be renewed interest. Try to avoid them pulling away sharply as this could cause pain; however, one or other do sometimes squeal as they release, often because of the shock. Talk gently, reassuring the pair and he will probably lie down to clean himself. Let him get on with that.

Both could dash about flirting, he may even lick her vulva; this is normal and gives a confident, pleasurable end to the event. It is very unlikely that he would genuinely be able to mate her again, but if he is getting too amorous just divert his attention with encouraging support. Be rewarding in your actions and words so he is aware that you approve, leaving him with positive thoughts about mating.

Some people feel that the dog's genitals should be doused with a mild antiseptic solution. We work on the principle that nature knows best, and the less unnecessary intervention the better.

Return both dogs to rest, him to his normal quarters, her to the car. Now everyone can retire to the house for coffee and paperwork, in the knowledge that it is a job well done.

OLD WIVES' TALES

A number of old wives' tales abound. Some make common sense, others are just daft, but if it works for you and it is not harming dog or human, then that is fine.

A stud dog can only mate one bitch a day to produce puppies.
This is a total fallacy. We have known more than one experienced stud dog which has mated up to four bitches in one day, either all producing puppies, or on one occasion the only bitch who missed having a litter was the first one. We might add that it is not common practice to use a dog this number of times in a day; it would only occur in extreme circumstances.

Hold up the hindquarters of the bitch on completion of the tie, to allow the sperm to run back into the bitch.
We truly cannot see the point of this; the pair has just been tied together for the last twenty minutes or so. This is also the case, where the owner feels the need to massage the belly of the bitch.

Don't let the bitch wee after mating.
She will not wee the sperm out. If the thinking is that urine can kill sperm, yes it can, but the sperm is well into the uterus by this time.

7 THE GESTATION PERIOD

Preparation of the bitch is essential before she is even mated. Indeed the whole kennel of dogs needs to be in good health and condition: this is basic good animal husbandry, and without this you should not even have a pet, and undoubtedly should not be considering breeding.

Vaccinations that may be due during gestation should be administered before the bitch is mated; similarly it is wise to have the worming programme completed before mating. It is probably best that this sort of process intrudes into the bitch's metabolism as little as possible at this time; however, having said that, many carry out these procedures during gestation with no ill effects.

Once the bitch has been mated, she must be kept securely away from other male dogs, as she may still be receptive to copulation. However, if more than one dog does inadvertently mate the bitch, it is easy to determine the parentage of offspring with the advent of DNA testing of dogs, which is encouraged by the Kennel Club. Nevertheless, obviously it is better if this does not occur.

A bitch in whelp is special, but does not need pampering: she should be treated as normal, though just be aware that the most vulnerable time for the fertilized eggs is before they attach to the uterus (before three weeks in whelp), so avoid too much change, which could cause

When pregnancy is advanced and her tummy is large, take care that the bitch is does not try to squeeze through small gaps, as she may not realize that she can't fit through.

stress. Owners often steer clear of taking a mated bitch to shows or dog-related events to avoid the risk of picking up infection. In those first three weeks, the bitch needs to avoid stress, another good reason to leave her in familiar surroundings and not risk absorption of the free-floating foetuses.

Otherwise continue with normal exercise: it is important that she remains fit and active, which will assist with the ease of birth. However, avoid activities she is not accustomed to.

Gestation is sixty-three days, whether the dog is a Great Dane or a Pomeranian. A maiden bitch will often have her puppies three days early.

It must be remembered that gestation is from when the eggs are fertilized, not when the bitch is actually mated: there can be a discrepancy between the two dates due to the fact that sperm can live for a number of days.

FEEDING

Bitches can go off their food, principally two to three weeks after conception, and can even suffer from morning sickness, just like many human mothers-to-be; in fact many symptoms are similar. If the bitch does become a picky eater, there is no need to be alarmed, rushing to 'tempt' her with tasty morsels, as this could lead to her only accepting this 'special' feeding regime, which of course is not conducive to a healthy diet for a pregnant bitch. Normal feeding habits will resume after whelping, and doubtless her appetite will increase to such a level that she will be ravenous, and could even steal food when previously her manners were impeccable.

A quality feed is easily obtained these days. Manufacturers are involved in a multi-million pound industry, and each product is carefully balanced to provide every nutrient needed to fulfil the requirements of the canine at every stage in its life, whether he is big, small, active or sedentary.

Everyone has very definite ideas on feeding dogs, and each thinks their own way is the best. To make sure your bitch is in optimum health, it may be necessary to give her a food with an increased protein level up to a month before she is mated, thus giving the eggs the best chance to be of good quality. A bitch in poor health, underweight or excessively fat will have less chance of having a correct sized litter, and her poor condition could also have a detrimental influence on foetus development.

Often the proprietary brands have a specific diet for pregnant and lactating bitches. It is worth chatting to your supplier, who can advise on the needs of your breed. If feeding a complete diet specific to your bitch's needs it is inadvisable to add, say, extra calcium, as too much can have a negative affect. Calcium, in particular, if given in excess can lead to pre-eclampsia or eclampsia, because it affects the normal processes of calcium storage within the body. Similarly too much vitamin A has been known to cause congenital problems, such as cleft palate.

The bitch needs to be fit but not too fat, as the latter could affect her fertility levels and cause her not to conceive. And once she has been mated, don't be under the impression that she needs 'feeding up', as having her too fat is conducive to problems, and could easily contribute to trouble when whelping. Her food intake should be increased further into her pregnancy.

At four to five weeks' gestation the whelps will be taking more nutrients from the bitch, so start increasing her food. By six weeks, the bitch will require one quarter more calories. At around seven weeks after conception, she will need roughly one-and-a-half times her normal ration.

Each breed is slightly different in its needs at this time, so use your eye to see if she is starting to look a little poor, if her ribs are showing or she is perhaps lacking condition on her back, in which case her food ration should be increased. Consider consulting an expert such as the breeder nutrition adviser or care line as connected to all the superior premium dog food manufacturers: they will fully advise on the individual needs of each breed.

It is important always to be observant throughout the pregnancy, keeping the potential 'mum' in optimum condition. Probably before, but definitely by eight weeks into the pregnancy, it will be better to start feeding three smaller meals, rather than two large ones. Because the growing whelps are taking up so much room, it is difficult for the dam actually to take enough food at one or two sittings.

During parturition, many bitches won't eat: this is fine, but make sure she is taking enough liquid. She will usually drink water, if it is a long and/or arduous labour, and she can be given a milk drink with glucose and even an egg included to give her energy. To really quench thirst, we would give a bowl of tea with glucose. Tea is also useful if puppies, or any dog, have a bout of diarrhoea: it is readily taken, (as it would be by a human feeling off colour) and rehydrates quickly.

At this time the bitch will be too busy with the delivery to think about taking food, and she will probably eat the placenta of the whelps, another reason she is not too interested in food.

SIGNS OF PREGNANCY

Once the single-celled eggs have been fertilized they will immediately start to divide; they are now known as blastocysts. If the bitch has had more than one mating some of the blastocysts may be older than others, but they will all migrate to the uterus at the same time and will implant into the uterine horns; this gives them stability. The blastocysts will now have developed a placenta, at approximately day twenty; it is impossible to confirm pregnancy before this time.

The placenta includes in its make-up some coagulated blood, and this degenerates over time, becoming green in colour; this is why during whelping the discharge left on the bedding is often green. This can alarm the breeder, and many people are under the impression that this green discharge is a sign of trouble; this is not the case, however, unless other worrying factors are present.

The attachment of the placenta also has the umbilical cord, which connects to the budding foetuses, supplying them with nourishment. Therefore it is imperative to make sure the pregnant bitch does not take in any potentially poisonous or harmful substances, as these will be administered to the foetus through her blood supply.

If a foetus dies, for whatever reason – possibly it is deformed or has defects – early in the pregnancy, it will be absorbed into the dam's tissues so there is no sign that it ever existed. Later in pregnancy, when the dead foetus is too advanced in development to be successfully absorbed, its expulsion would most likely result in abortion; uterine infection might also result from the decaying dead matter, if all is not expelled.

Your vet should be consulted before administering any drugs or additives.

Phantom Pregnancies
In the early stages of pregnancy, a breeder who knows their established line may recognize signs that are characteristic to the strain; however they are usually wise enough not to voice their assumptions too early, as the signs may be there but the bitch could be having a false pregnancy, showing many signs of being in whelp, only to revert to her normal shape late in the so-called 'gestation'. In a severe false pregnancy she can lactate heavily, even to the point of developing mastitis, which would require veterinary intervention. This is extreme, but many bitches act as if they have puppies, cuddling a squeaky toy, in fact often guarding it. They may dig up the garden or want to stay in their bed. All these behaviours are to be discouraged, and it is advisable to increase the bitch's stimulation and activity levels to give her another interest.

Early Stages of Pregnancy
Signs that the bitch probably is in whelp manifest themselves as follows: she can become quieter than normal, and a little 'precious'. She will need to urinate more than normal: you might find a puddle on the kitchen or kennel floor in the morning, when normally she is clean. Don't scold her, as she can't help this; she will return to being clean at around four weeks in whelp. Later in the pregnancy this will happen again, because as the puppies grow and fill the uterus, this will put pressure on her bladder and she will need to wee more often.

During the early part of gestation, the bitch could have a clear creamy discharge: this is normal, and should not cause concern.

Approaching the three-week period: The bitch's mammary glands may be more noticeable, the teats will become pink

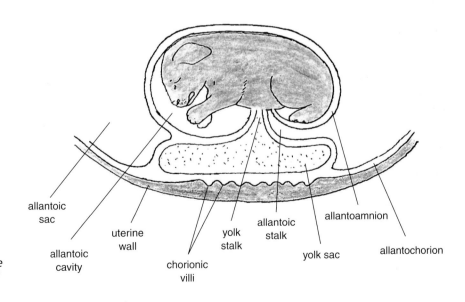

The structure of the foetal unit.

allantoic sac

uterine wall

allantoic cavity

chorionic villi

yolk stalk

allantoic stalk

yolk sac

allantoamnion

allantochorion

and stand erect, and she could become picky in her eating habits; it is even possible that she could suffer with morning sickness. Other than these symptoms, bodily she won't change much; it is not wise to overfeed her, as you don't want her too overweight, therefore feed to maintain condition but not to put fat on to her ribs. If it turns out that she is not in whelp you could end up with an obese dog, and extra weight is hard to budge. Alternatively, if she is in whelp and is carrying excessive fat, she has to carry this around as well as the growing whelps, which will put added stress on her heart and frame.

Determining Pregnancy

At around four weeks' gestation: An experienced breeder, or more probably the vet, will often be able to feel the uterine swellings – the foetuses – in an average-sized bitch, following palpation of the flank area behind the ribs. Be aware that it is risky to try this method if you are inexperienced, as you could do more harm than good. Furthermore, detection is not so easy in small breeds, or breeds that are particularly short, as the foetuses can be tucked up in the rib area. In short, this is no guarantee of pregnancy, and I don't know of any vet who will definitively affirm pregnancy following this type of examination – he will just give an informed indication.

After about four and a half weeks into pregnancy the foetuses grow rapidly and they will not be able to be detected in this way.

The altogether more efficient way of determining pregnancy is by ultrasound: sophisticated equipment is becoming more readily available, and more practised technicians make for more accurate results. For best results the area to be scanned should be shaved, particularly if dealing with a long- or double-coated breed. This technology is non-invasive and therefore causes no risk or pain either to bitch or foetuses. As a result the bitch will generally stand easily whilst the ultrasound is performed. Sound-wave imaging detects the foetus, and the added advantage is that if used on or after the fourth week, it will show the heartbeat.

If the bitch is having a large litter it is difficult to see all the foetuses, so ultrasound is generally used to determine pregnancy rather than the exact number of puppies due.

A blood test can be used to confirm that the bitch is in whelp; however, this is not used very often these days, as other methods are easier and more predictable. Using X-ray to determine pregnancy is not a good option as there is a certain amount of risk with this method, and it should only be performed by a qualified practitioner if it is felt essential to the wellbeing of mother and whelps. X-ray is generally only used during whelping to determine if any foetuses or placenta are left, which could cause infection to the bitch.

At around four to five weeks' gestation: The shape of the bitch starts to change. If viewed from above, instead of appearing concave at the waist – the back of the ribs below the loin – it will look thicker, and her waist will have evened out with the spring of her ribs, which will have developed more to accommodate the growing puppies. This is evident earlier in small breeds, as the bitch has less room in the rib cavity for the puppies.

At six to seven weeks: It will be more noticeable that the bitch is pregnant. Her spine is likely to feel raised when you run your hand down her back, and the bitch

PREPARING THE WHELPING AREA

It is now time to think about buying or making a whelping box. It is not a good idea to borrow a whelping box, as this will lead to cross-infection of germs. If you already have a box, give it an extra thorough clean with a disinfectant, and leave it outside in the weather for a couple of days. Then wash it again and take it into the whelping area to dry thoroughly. This way it is as germ free as possible, and ready to be put in place for the impending birth.

A home-made wooden whelping box is cheap, and easily made and disposed of, thus removing the spread of disease. It is lined with fleece bedding and a heat lamp is positioned overhead.

carrying a large-sized litter will have an even more prominent backbone, even though she is not underweight. This is a sure sign of pregnancy, because a bitch having a false pregnancy will not show this symptom, even though she might have the other indications.

It is important at this stage to increase her feed, and to feed by splitting meals; much of her nourishment at this stage will be going to feed the growing puppies.

In a coated breed, at six weeks' gestation you may notice that the hair on her flank curls up, another reliable sign of pregnancy. This is probably because of the change in her shape as her belly starts to fill out. If she is healthy and adequately fed, her coat will gleam with wellbeing even more than normal.

Sometimes it is not apparent that she has other outward indications, even in a short-coated breed; she could still retain the tuck-up at the back of her ribs visible in her underline, however it is probable that her underline will start to bulge and drop.

By eight weeks: She will definitely have a growing belly. She will be uncomfortable, and will be grateful for cosier bedding. A bitch at eight to nine weeks' gestation will often lie on her back for a time, displaying her swollen tummy and defined mammary glands; this seems to give her relief from the discomfort of the growing whelps. It is fascinating to watch her belly at this time, as the puppies can be clearly seen moving around, especially with a large litter, since things are probably fairly cramped in there!

Now is the time to move the bitch to the prepared whelping box. Put the heating on if necessary, making sure it is at a consistent temperature, and check for draughts. This allows her time to become

A heavily pregnant bitch will often lie on her back, which provides relief from discomfort.

The expectant bitch uses the whelping box to rest in a week before due date, and so will not be stressed by this environment during partition.

accustomed to the new surroundings, so she feels less stress at parturition.

During the ninth week: A close eye must be kept on the bitch: it is not that unusual for a maiden bitch to whelp three days early, at sixty days. Many breeders have experience of a bitch giving birth a full week early, with healthy puppies born – this is not a regular occurrence, but be prepared.

Alternatively she could go over her due time, which can be worrying: how long to leave her before you become concerned? If in doubt always consult your vet, who will be happy to check the bitch over to make sure all is well. Of course no one is foolproof, and if you know your bitch's normal habits when having puppies and your instinct is warning you of impending trouble, voice this to your vet. The vet, who knows you well, will be happy to have knowledge of a previous whelping, or of the usual habits of a particular family line – when a breeder has an established line of bitches sometimes a pattern can emerge, and I have seen this happen in other species of animal too, 'Like mother, like daughter'.

Watch the bitch carefully, as she may

want to slope off upstairs to find a comfortable bed to dig up in preparation of whelping, or to tunnel holes in the garden in which to hide her new family.

SIGNS OF GIVING BIRTH

As the bitch approaches her time to give birth, the muscles around her vulva and back end will appear slack and floppy. She will naturally have started to take things more steadily through the later stages of her pregnancy: she will know her limitations. However, don't allow her to jump over things or to push past or through narrow gaps – she may try to do these things, not realizing that her body won't go through without potential damage to the puppies. Earlier in her pregnancy the foetuses are well protected by the fluid sack that encases them.

DEVELOPMENT OF THE PUPPIES DURING GESTATION

The normal development of gestation is separated into three phases:

1. Pre-implantation, day one to about day fourteen.
2. Embryogenesis, day fourteen to roughly day thirty.
3. Foetal growth, from day thirty approximately to birth.

It can only be approximate, because the sperm can live for up to a week in the bitch's reproductive tract before fertilization, therefore exact conception is hard to predict.

As stated earlier, the embryo is implanted in the uterus at about three weeks gestation. Before this the eggs are floating free, which makes them vulnera-

SCALE OF FOETUS DEVELOPMENT

Week 1 (1–7 days): Fertilization of the eggs, following mating. Two-cell embryos are in the oviduct. The embryos are fairly resistant to external interference at this time.

Week 2 (8–14 days): At the start of this week the embryos will be four cells; by the end of this period they will have multiplied to sixty-four.

Week 3 (15–21 days): Around day nineteen the embryos will be implanted in the uterus.

Week 4 (22–28 days): The foetuses are growing now. The eyes start to develop and the face takes shape. The spinal cord is developing. At this time the embryo is susceptible to defects.

Week 5 (29–35 days): At this point the foetus starts to look like a puppy. Toes are forming, claws and whisker buds. The gender of the puppy is determined. The previously open eyes will now close. Organogenesis ends, leaving the embryo now fairly resistant to interference in development.

Week 6 (36–42 days): The pigment in the skin is evident, and the heartbeat can be detected with the use of a stethoscope.

Week 7 (43–49 days): General growth and development continues.

Week 8 (50–57 days): The puppies are active and can be seen under the skin of the bitch moving around. Delivery can produce healthy puppies at this time.

Week 9 (58–65 days): The puppies continue to grow; at around sixty days they will have a full coat of hair with fully formed pads and nails. The body is covered in touch-sensitive nerve endings.

The bitch will prepare for parturition by nesting; she will pant, and possibly go off her food, and her body temperature will become lower.

ble to damage at this stage, and if damage is incurred the embryo is likely to die and be absorbed.

Between the second and fourth week, embryonic tissue and organs are sensitive to interference. Make sure that the bitch receives a balanced diet, avoiding any excess of vitamins as this can cause defects in the foetus.

The Importance of Temperature

In the womb, the puppies are at a constant temperature of 38.6°C (101.5°F), but when the bitch is nearing parturition her body temperature will become lower, possibly to accustom the puppies to the lower temperature in the new world they are to enter. Delivery should take place within about twenty-four hours of her temperature dropping from normal, 38.5°C (100.2–100.8°F) to 37.05°C (98–99.4°F).

As the puppies are born the mother will lick each newborn energetically, not only to help clean and dry it, but to stimulate its body and senses into action. This helps the puppy breathe properly and its body to generate heat.

Following the stress of birth, the puppy is more vulnerable to hypothermia and infection, which is why direct heat from a lamp is useful; the lamp should be positioned high enough to allow the mother to stand without touching it. The fleecy, rubber-backed bedding generates warmth, allowing the birth fluids to pass through, keeping mother and babies comfortable. Placing the whelping box in a draught-free, quiet place will minimize stress for the bitch, which would pass on to the whelps.

If a puppy is found to be cold and at risk of dying, the quickest way of bringing its body temperature back to normal is to submerge the puppy in a container of water at blood heat (regulate the water temperature carefully, to avoid scalding), keeping the head above the water. Dry the puppy with a warm towel and pop him on a teat. It is amazing how well this works.

Working with animals means we must be in empathy with nature, and it never ceases to amaze even the most experienced breeder that newborn puppies will instantly start shuffling round to the teat and drinking for all they are worth, born with the need to eat or die!

8 THE BIRTH

Gestation in a canine is sixty-three days, according to the 'book'. However, we are working with Nature here, so we have to go with what she says. There is a tendency for toy breeds to be earlier, and some of the giant breeds can go over this time regularly, to no ill effect. We once had a bitch that really had no signs that she was going to have puppies, and a full week later had six! Likewise we have had a bitch that whelped a full week early, showing no signs the evening before: we found her in the morning lying contentedly with her babies. This is not the norm, however, and in the breeds that we have owned and whelped, a bitch is usually three days early when having her first litter.

A bitch having a large litter can often deliver early, and multiple puppies tend to speed up the whelping process as they are close together in the horns of the uterus and move forwards one after the other. However, if the bitch is really heavy with puppies and they are big, she may not be able to get started, and may need the vet. In the same way one puppy can be a problem in that the single whelp is often big, and delivery is hampered by the fact that the puppy just stays there – again, veterinary interception may be required. If the bitch is very unsettled, panting dramatically, and appears distressed, this could mean veterinary intervention is needed. If she starts to push (bear down) but is not delivering a

puppy within a good half hour, again seek veterinary advice.

It is better to be sure than sorry.

THE WHELPING QUARTERS

Serious breeders will have whelping quarters made of brick or block, and rendered (this makes maintenance and cleaning much more efficient). These 'nursery' kennels will be in a separate unit from the normal kennels where all the other dogs are kept; it is therefore away from the inquisitive eyes of the other dogs, it can be cleaned thoroughly and 'rested' between whelpings so that disease does not build up, kept at a constant temperature, and most importantly is quiet, so the new family remains undisturbed.

The whelping unit should have a kennel or kennels of a size that comfortably contains the whelping box, with enough space for the mother to come out of it and lie outside away from the puppies, and also have a drink of water. This kennel will furthermore serve as a run for the puppies to play in when they are older, and can also be used as a lavatory as it can be cleaned easily, since naturally the puppies will not want to dirty their sleeping area. Having a kennel for the puppies to grow up in gives them peace and quiet, therefore they rest, which is indispensable for growth and development, just as for a human baby.

The 'nursery' kennel will have been previously prepared, so that after whelping, mum and puppies can rest in a quiet, draught-free environment.

The theory that puppies need plenty of stimulation to be social in later life is true; however, when puppies are reared in the house, every distraction wakes them, whether it is the vacuum, telephone, doorbell or visitors. Think about how human babies are reared: they will be cuddled, fed and interacted with, but then put somewhere quiet to sleep for a large segment of the day.

The whelping box can be cheaply and easily made from wood. It should be big enough for the bitch to lie flat out in, but not so big that the puppies move too far from her, or she will spend time getting up to bring them back close to her – and each time she lies back down a puppy risks being squashed and suffocated. Ideally the sides will be high enough so that mum can't get under the edge, with a lip turned in, about the width of a 4in

(10cm) plank for a large dog, or 3in (7.5cm) for a smaller dog, so if a puppy sleeps at the edge of the whelping box, the mother will not lie on it. Because the box is cheap to make it can be burned after use, thus reducing the spread of infection.

It is good practice to put the whelping box in place a couple of weeks before the bitch is due. This gives her time to know that this is her place, where she can prepare for the birth. Also, if caught off guard and parturition comes early, everything is organized. Used newspaper is very absorbent, and collecting the daily paper ahead of time gives a stock for the messy process of whelping.

Also the fleece bedding which is readily available these days is excellent as another layer to place on the newspaper: it is absorbent, excess liquid passes through, it is very warm, and it gives grip to the bitch during parturition and to whelps before they are able to walk. It does not ruff up into a ball during whelping when the mother is scratching around, so puppies are not caught under the blankets and lain on, and it can be washed numerous times in the washer on a hot cycle. So it works out as very economical.

A heat lamp may be placed above the box: it must be high enough so as not to burn either bitch or whelps, and so the bitch doesn't touch the lamp if she stands up, but low enough to provide adequate heat at a constant temperature. It is important that this constant temperature is maintained and that there are no draughts, as new puppies have no heat control and would die without warmth. The ideal environmental temperature should be around 27–30°C (80–86°F).

We generally take the bitch into the house to have her pups, as she will often have them in the early hours of the morning when it is quiet. In the wild, predators would be asleep, so she can concentrate on her job without fear. Obviously for us it is easier to keep an eye on her in the comfort of the kitchen, rather than in a kennel. Once the puppies are born and a close eye kept on the proceedings to make sure all whelps are sucking heartily, the new family can be moved into the quiet puppy kennel. If kept in the kitchen or house, the new family could be troubled by all the comings and goings that affect the normal running of a home. It is very difficult to stop people from peeping at the puppies, especially children, and even the sweetest-natured bitch may not take kindly to this lack of respect of her space.

If possible, try to just oversee the birth, rather than rushing in anxious to help. Nature has a marvellous way of making sure that the mother's instinct will tell her what to do.

PARTURITION

Parturition takes place in a three stage sequence: preparing for parturition, the birth itself, and expelling the afterbirth.

Stage One: Preparing for Parturition
A few days before birth the bitch's hindquarters will appear slack around the pelvic area, though for the novice owner this may be hard to determine. As the time for parturition comes closer, the vulva will soften and swell in preparation for the birth of the puppies. The mother will probably try to get to part of the garden and start digging furiously, instinctively trying to find a safe place to have her puppies. People say that usually a day before parturition, a bitch will not want to eat. However, this is not the case with our breed, Weimaraners, which will eat between whelps!

The bitch will become restless, scrabbling around and digging up her bedding. Often she will fidget about and shake as contractions increase. She might take exception to the whelping box and whine to go upstairs so that she can have her puppies on your bed. Some people allow their bitch to have the first puppy where she wants, just to get things started. We would firmly but kindly make her realize that this is unacceptable behaviour – remember, as a pack animal you must be considered pack leader. She will ultimately take reassurance from your confident attitude. It is wise to keep general onlookers out of the way, though, so as to respect her need for peace at this time. One should be even more vigilant when a bitch is a maiden (has not had a litter before).

To prepare the body for birth in this first stage, the uterine muscle forms contractions, which dilate the uterus and lubricate and relax the passage the puppy will take to be born.

All this can take either a day or so, or it might be over quite quickly, in a matter of hours. If your bitch is a heavily coated breed it is wise to clip the hair from around the hindquarters – it is pointless thinking she will retain her coat. All bitches go through a moult between about four and ten weeks after whelping, so no matter how attentive you are with cleaning and grooming, the coat will invariably drop out.

As the bitch progresses through labour, she will become more uncomfortable and will want to go out often to relieve herself, in preparation for the birth. This is nature's way of making sure the bitch has emptied herself before she starts bearing down to have a puppy: it is 'Nature's enema'.

The most obvious real sign of impending parturition is that the mother's temperature will drop. While the normal temperature for a dog is 37.7–38°C (100–100.5°F), this will drop to about 36.6°C (98°F).

Stage Two: The Birth Itself

As labour increases, it will become more obvious that things are starting to become imminent. Contractions will show by the bitch 'paining' at increasing intervals. She will pant and lick her vulva repeatedly; she will stand up, turn round and generally try to place herself in an efficient position whereby she can give birth. Her waters will break, when a fairly clear liquid will squirt from the vulva – no reason for alarm at this stage.

Once she starts bearing down – pushing – you need to keep a note of the time, because if this stage goes on for too long without any further development, it could result in complications. If a birth has not occurred within a good half-an-hour, take her out and see if this will 'stir things up'. A trot round the garden can often do the trick. However, if this doesn't work, consult your vet, stating how long she has been straining strongly.

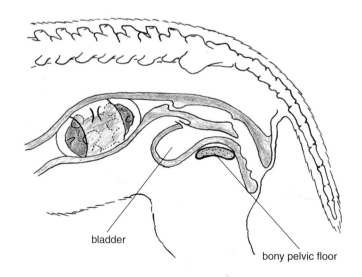

The first puppy, still enclosed in its sac, awaits the second stage of birth.

bladder

bony pelvic floor

In the later stages of labour, as her contractions increase, the bitch 'pains' and will chew on something for relief.

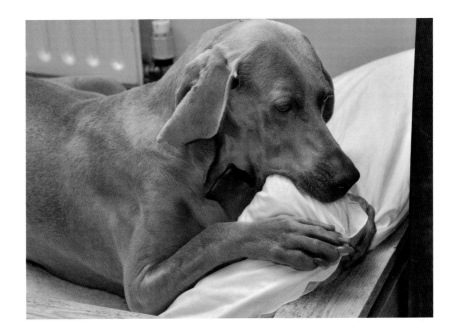

The vet may suggest taking her along to the surgery, for various reasons: first, the car journey can help the puppy to be born – it is amazing how many puppies are born at the side of a busy road. Second, if the puppy is stuck it is better to be at the surgery where the vet has everything he needs to hand. Usually a puppy sticks at the pelvic area, due to the bone structure being fixed and therefore unyielding. The vet may need to use forceps to deliver a puppy that is wedged, or he may feel that the mother needs oxytocin. The vet often uses this drug in conjunction with whelping, if problems arise.

Oxytocin will initiate strong, regular and purposeful contractions of the uterine muscle, especially if the bitch experiences uterine inertia (the inability to contract, which stops puppies being born, due to tiredness following a long arduous labour). Oxytocin is also helpful in promoting involution of the post-parturi-

ent uterus, thus helping the passage of any retained placenta, and it will encourage milk production – 'letting the milk down'.

Thirdly, if all else fails the bitch could need a Caesarean section, which obviously needs to be done at the surgery, by the vet, under general anaesthesia. (Whelping difficulties will be explained more specifically later.)

So as labour progresses and normal delivery proceeds, the first puppy will present itself through the vulva encased in the foetal membranes; the umbilical cord, through which the puppy gained nutrients from the mother, will still be attached to the placenta. The first sign of imminent birth will probably be the membrane forming a bubble from the vulva. This may burst, but the puppy will not drown or smother, as the cord is still attached.

The normal presentation of a puppy is nose and front feet first: this is because,

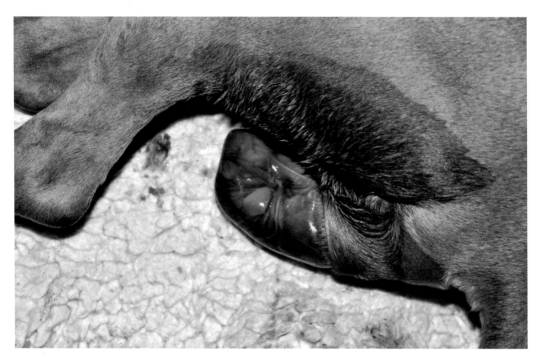

A puppy emerging in its foetal membrane.

when the front legs are positioned forwards and the head placed in the direction it is going, the circumference of the puppy will be at its smallest in readiness to be ejected through the pelvic girdle. However, it is not unusual to see a tail poking out – though be careful not to pull a puppy out by his tail, as you might just pull it off!

People can be upset by a breech presentation, but we have found no problems with this presentation in canines, as long as the puppy is not stuck in this position. It can be a little trickier if just the tail is evident, as this leaves a larger-than-normal area of puppy to be delivered. In animals where only one young is born, the foetus is generally large, and this can be a problem. If the legs were back they would have to be brought forwards before birth could be completed, risking suffocation. The bitch will lick her hindquarters and often stand in a crouched position as she is bearing down.

The first whelp born may alarm the bitch if she is a maiden, so watch that she doesn't bite it – or indeed you – as a result of the stress and pain she may be feeling. If needs be, at this stage, you can firmly but gently grip the puppy with your thumb and forefinger and ease it into the world. If helping to deliver a whelp, hold the puppy and gently pull, but only when the mother is actually having a contraction. If the head is causing the obstruction, carefully run a forefinger around the head, easing it forwards so that the puppy will then be able to slip out.

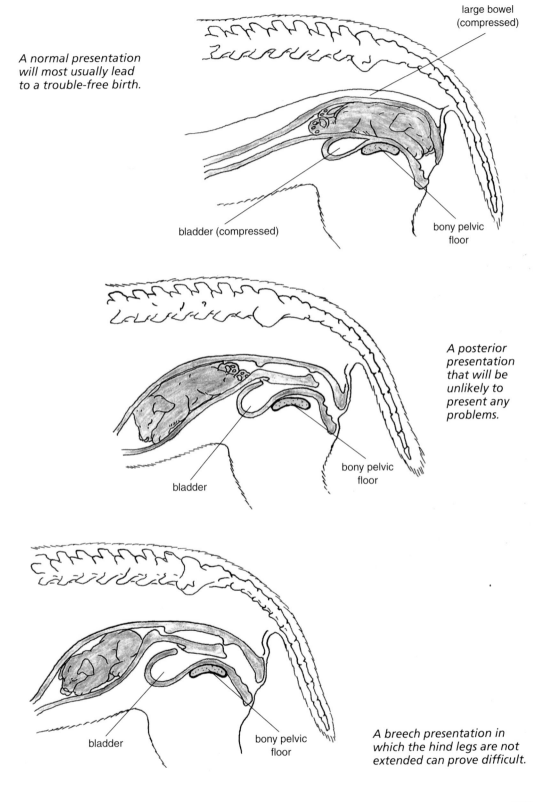

A normal presentation will most usually lead to a trouble-free birth.

large bowel (compressed)

bladder (compressed)

bony pelvic floor

A posterior presentation that will be unlikely to present any problems.

bladder

bony pelvic floor

bladder

bony pelvic floor

A breech presentation in which the hind legs are not extended can prove difficult.

An otherwise normal
presentation, in which
a withdrawn foreleg
and a turned head
might cause problems.

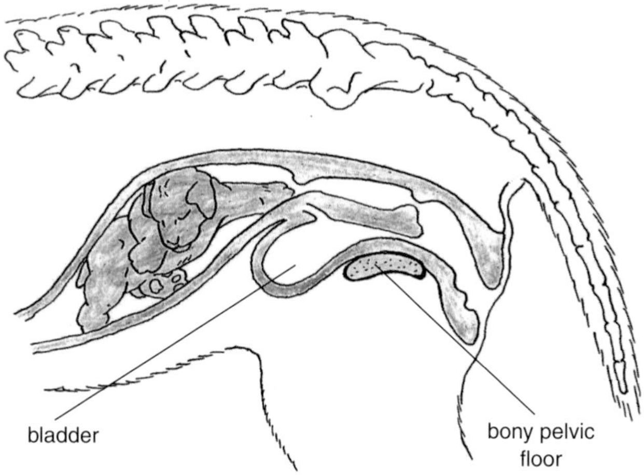

bladder

bony pelvic
floor

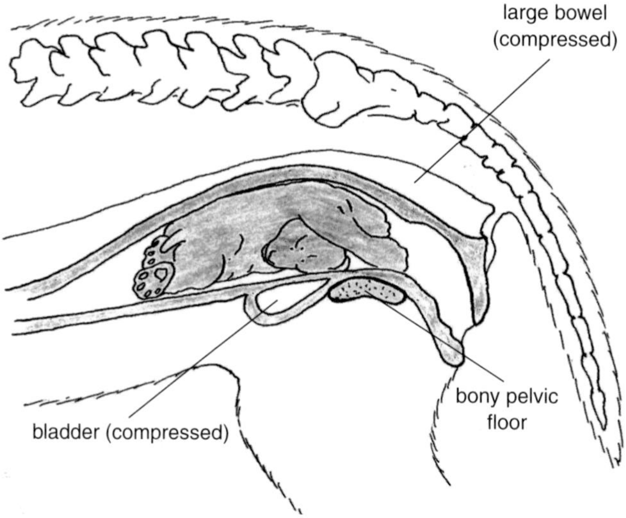

large bowel
(compressed)

Flexion of the
head may
obstruct a
normal birth.

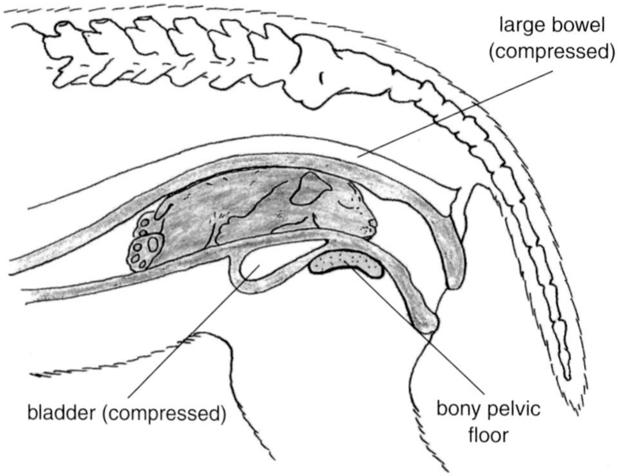

bladder (compressed)

bony pelvic
floor

large bowel
(compressed)

bladder (compressed)

bony pelvic
floor

Head forward and forelimbs
deflected will make the
shoulder bulge and create
an obstruction.

RIGHT: *As the puppy enters the world, mum will clean the 'sac', allowing the puppy to breathe.*

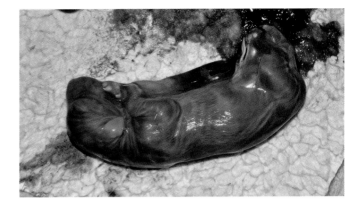

BELOW: *With the umbilical cord severed, mum can settle down to lick the puppy, stimulating circulation.*

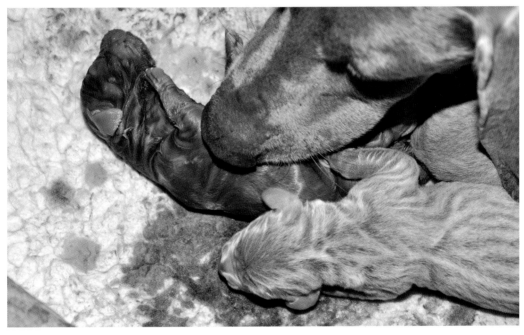

As the puppy emerges he will be encased in a sac: in an ideal world, the mother should break this open and chew through the cord, licking him vigorously to stimulate his circulation and 'shock' him into breathing. Oversee this initially, and if she is lethargic in her attempt to fulfil this duty, you must intervene. Rupture the sac, making sure the puppy's nose and mouth are clear so that he can breathe, and remove it from the body. It is often thought that the cord should be cut with sterile scissors, but we would sever the cord with the thumbnail, taking care not to pull the cord away from the body, which could cause a hernia. If the cord is cut it makes a sharp-edged entry that is open to infection, whereas if it is broken with the nails, as the mother would do with her teeth, the cord is sealed closed.

Briskly, but not harshly, rub the puppy with a clean towel to stimulate it. Put it near the mother's mouth so that she knows it is hers, and encourage her to lick it. This will start the bonding process and settle her a little. At the other extreme she may be over-zealous in cleaning him, and may pick him up and try to carry him off to a safe place – when of course she must be told, firmly and gently, that this is not acceptable.

This can be a tedious time whilst she has only one puppy, but she will settle down when she has puppy number two. Generally, though, once the first puppy is born and starting to suck, the mother will settle down and begin to clean it, licking its genitals and thereby stimulating it to pass urine and faeces.

Stage Three: Expelling the Afterbirth

Stage three tends to merge with stage two, because after a puppy is delivered, uterine contractions often continue in order to expel the placenta or afterbirth. This will often happen after each puppy, though the afterbirths may be retained until after all the puppies are born. It is often difficult to know if the afterbirth has been passed, as the mother is instinctively fastidious and will eat it, a biological capability left over from the wild when it was imperative to leave no trace, therefore reducing the risk of predators looking for an easy meal.

Do not be alarmed if the discharge during birth is dark green as well as containing blood; this is normal, after the first puppy. If, however, it happens before any births, it could mean that the placenta of the first puppy has severed from the wall of the uterus, in which case the puppy itself could be being starved of oxygen and needs to be born quickly – so don't hesitate to act.

GENERAL OBSERVATIONS

The time between whelps varies dramatically. If you are very lucky you could find only half an hour or less between whelps, yet sometimes four or five hours can pass between births. If the mother is not too distressed, and not pushing heartily, everything is probably fine. However, if you are at all unsure, contact your vet: again, it is better to be safe than sorry.

We once had a bitch that whelped seven healthy pups and settled down at about five o'clock. She went out to relieve herself and stretch her legs, then ate her supper, all being well. The next morning I looked into the whelping box, counted eight, checked again, rubbed my eyes – and yes, she had delivered another healthy puppy! Considering I had not taken to my bed until 3am, the puppy was ten hours after his siblings, with no ill effects!

As I suggested earlier, whelping often takes place in the middle of the night, so you should always have a torch at the ready. If the bitch needs/wants to go out in the night, she may squat to relieve herself and pass a puppy – and how devastating it would be to find a dead puppy in the morning light.

If the mother is not getting on with delivery and there is a long time between whelps, it might be useful to get her out of the whelping box and take her out. This may necessitate putting a lead on her and physically taking her out, as she will not want to leave the nest. Upon taking her out you often find she is actually desperate to wee, so it is important that you do make sure that she is taken out regularly: if left too long she could develop a urinary infection. Watch how careful she is when returning to her babies; this will give a good indication as

During birth the bedding becomes soiled and very wet. For comfort and hygiene, change it when someone takes mum out to stretch her legs.

to how she will be when left to get on with looking after her litter, and above all not lying on the puppies.

During parturition an amazing amount of fluid is discharged, so whilst someone is out in the garden with the mother, have another person take out the fouled fleece bedding and wet newspaper and replace it with fresh; this makes her more comfortable, and of course it is a matter of hygiene.

The bitch will be tired with all the exer- tion of whelping, so make sure she is offered water regularly. If she is not eager to drink, a cup of tea with glucose will usually be taken and will give her energy, or a bowl of milk with an egg whisked in it. It is essential that she has fluids, be it water or other drinks, as this will help her milk production.

When is Parturition Complete?
A whose bitch was friend having her first litter asked Stephen this question.

Mum and puppies relaxed and content on clean, warm bedding.

Puppies thriving and satisfied is a truly wonderful sight.

His reply was, 'That's easy. If you pick up the final born and look closely at its tail…' 'Yes,' she replied, doing just that, and Stephen continued, 'It will have written along the tail, "The end!"' If it were only that simple!

Experienced breeders instinctively know when a bitch has finished, however, by gently but determinedly manipulating the gut – perhaps when she is out in the garden – it is possible to feel if there is something hard still in her, which would be another puppy. If there isn't, when she returns to the whelping box she will lie down contentedly, all the puppies sucking, making a truly wonderful sight.

Sometimes she will show all the signs of being finished, but unless you are sure that all is done and all afterbirths have come away, have a word with the vet, who may suggest that an injection of Oxytocin be given, just to make certain. This would be administered by the vet. Oxytocin is a hormone solution that can stimulate contractions when a bitch has inertia; it also helps the bitch to expel any retained afterbirths, and instigates the 'let-down' of milk in the dam.

Some say that the bitch should not be allowed to eat the afterbirths, but quite frankly they will do her no harm. It is a natural process.

The puppies will soon dry off, and you can then see whether all are healthy. They should be weighed: it is useful to make a log of their growth rate and development, how the bitch copes with her brood, and so on. This log can be a useful reference for future litters.

The Initial Nurture of Puppies

It is important that newborn puppies have the mother's first milk, colostrum; this milk contains antibodies, which protect the pup against infection and disease. If a puppy is reluctant to suck, put your finger and thumb each side of the mouth and squeeze the mouth open, then with the other hand squirt milk from the teat into his mouth: once he has tasted the milk he will generally get the idea and suck; if he continues to be a little slow, regularly repeat this procedure until he gains a little strength and he should start to feed.

If a puppy is not feeding or milk appears to be coming down the nose, it could have a cleft palate. There can be a hereditary element involved in this condition, so if it occurs, it would be wise not to breed from the dam again. This condition is most distressing, as the puppy appears perfect. On closer inspection of the roof of the mouth a split can be visibly seen. The puppy will have to be put to sleep to save suffering, except in extremely mild cases. Fortunately this is not a condition seen in breeds I have or am involved with, but I have seen cases in cocker spaniels and other breeds.

In our experience, working mainly with medium to large breeds, we have more uniformity in puppies in larger litters. They seem to even out and find a teat, and stick to the same teat, developing a routine. In fact each puppy generally sticks to the same teat. This would be nature's way of stopping problems such as mastitis, which can be caused by milk left in the udder. If a puppy sucks just 'his' teat, the teats not in use will dry up and cause no problems.

When we have had litters of three puppies, one will be a big bruiser, one average and one small, and they never seem to have any uniformity until much later in life, when the small one can catch up. The breeds we are involved with are recognized as basically healthy, so not many abnormalities are prevalent.

POTENTIAL ABNORMALITIES

If the puppy has an internal abnormality, it often shows itself after a day or two. An otherwise healthy-looking puppy will not be thriving, it will look dull and dehydrated and be apart from the others, away in a corner, generally put there by the mother: in the wild if a puppy is not right, she would push it away so as not to compromise the healthy ones. Try as you will, this puppy is doomed, and although it is always upsetting to lose a puppy,

Puppies need to be checked regularly to make sure that all is well.

nature must be treated with respect. However, this is a rare occurrence.

An interesting point is that pedigree breeds are born with definite characteristics of that breed. Right from when a puppy is cajoled into life by its mother, it shows signs of what it is, despite being blind and deaf at this stage. For example a strong, determined breed, such as the Weimaraner, will scrabble to the teat as the mother is cleaning him up; the terrier pup will busy around until he finds the teat, while the gentle, inoffensive English Setter will lie squealing until someone shows him where the teat is and what to do with it. This is not meant offensively: I have loved and lived with English Setters for some time.

PARTURITION DIFFICULTIES

Inertia

Inertia can be caused by the bitch being in poor physical condition, and therefore not strong enough to push. It can also be that she is unhappy in the environment she is in, which is why she should have the whelping box put in the place she is expected to deliver the puppies a good time before whelping, so she is relaxed there.

If the bitch is huge and obviously having a very large litter, this may cause inertia, as the puppies are so tightly packed they just cannot move out. The other cause is when the bitch is so exhausted that she is no longer able to push: in effect her system shuts down.

Whatever the cause, it is essential that the vet is informed and she is taken to the surgery for diagnosis. The vet may suggest Oxytocin, though more probably surgery will be needed in the form of a Caesarean section; this operation will be performed under a general anaesthetic,

so will be a last resort. Most vets will tell you to go home and they will ring you when all is finished. If you are allowed to stay, you could be a great help in stimulating the puppies as they are delivered. The puppies will also have had some anaesthetic through the mother and may be a little lethargic, so it will take quite a bit of work to get them going.

The vet will make an insertion along the length of the tummy between the teats, and will remove the puppies from one horn of the uterus, and then repeat this procedure with the other horn. If he has plenty of staff he will probably not want you present, and the nurse will work on the puppies; almost certainly you will be emotionally affected by your bitch having an operation, so it is better if you are not in attendance. A proficient vet will have administered just enough anaesthetic so that the bitch will be almost coming round as he is stitching her up.

When you take her home, the puppies will have been put in a carrying box with a hot water bottle to keep their temperature at the correct level, an important factor. When you arrive home make sure you have help available, as the bitch will need careful monitoring; she should be situated in her whelping box and restrained whilst the puppies are suckled on to her.

She will probably be disorientated and still suffering the aftereffects of the anaesthetic, and so may act out of character. She may not even know she has given birth, and may not want to lie still or let the puppies suckle, and could want to pick a puppy up; this could cause her to bite it too hard, injuring it even fatally. This sounds dramatic, but I know of a case where just such a situation occurred. The bitch picked up the puppy, but not appreciating her own strength, closed her teeth, ripping its tummy open; the puppy had to be put to sleep, and as it was an only one, the bitch was anxious for days. A harrowing event, that in addition cost a lot in monetary terms.

After a few hours mum will be fully round and in control of her faculties. When she starts to clean the puppies' genitals, all should be well and she can be observed from a distance as normal.

Stillbirth

It is distressing when an otherwise perfect-looking puppy is delivered dead. By the law of averages this is going to happen at some point when breeding, with no apparent causes. As with human babies, sometimes something is wrong congenitally, or the puppy was starved of oxygen in the womb, or some other malady.

Occasionally a puppy appears to be dead, but by rubbing him hard, even blowing softly into his mouth and tenderly massaging his heart with the thumb and forefinger, you can sometimes make him breathe and live. We have worked on a puppy for up to twenty minutes and actually saved it, with no ill effects. It merits a try, you have nothing to lose.

One interesting detail: a higher number of dog puppies are born, 103, to bitch puppies, 100. However, mortality tends to be higher in male puppies, so again nature has her way of addressing the balance.

Coping with Large Litters

In an exceptionally large litter, there is a theory that the weaker puppies should be culled – put to sleep – to give the stronger puppies a chance to thrive more readily. I feel strongly that this is 'playing God' and should not be an option. One of the best litters we reared had fourteen puppies. We were vigilant in our awareness of the growth and development of this litter, and with the smaller puppies, each time we passed and the puppies were sleeping, we would wake the smaller ones and put them on the mother's teats. All the puppies survived and grew into excellent specimens of the breed, three becoming champions and one gaining a certificate of merit in a field trial; and the ones we heard of in later life, lived well into double figures. We never hand fed the puppies: the mother made enough milk to feed all the whelps, as nature intended. If you start hand feeding, the puppies do not suckle on the mother as strongly, therefore she does not make as much milk.

The vet once suggested that a newly whelped bitch of ours had no milk and the puppies should be hand reared; however, we suckled the babies on often and gave the mother the obligatory cup of tea, and three hours later the puppies were full and settled, and never looked back.

You must trust your vet, but remember vets see dogs when something is amiss and rarely whelp a bitch in a normal birth, nor does a vet rear puppies. A bitch with what looks like a small udder can make as much, if not more milk, as a bitch with her teats hanging nearly to the floor. I am convinced that a bitch will make enough milk that is needed for her litter, and in thirty-seven years of breeding dogs and twenty years previous to that farming, I have never had evidence to the contrary. Maybe we have been extraordinarily lucky, but we have never hand reared a puppy when the bitch was alive and fit.

I once had a visitor who explained that she must return home quickly as she had a litter of four Cavalier King Charles Spaniels at five days old to hand feed; I asked if the bitch had no milk, and she explained that the mother did have milk, but the quality of the milk was poor, even though the mother was healthy. I supposed that the puppies had something amiss and would surely die – and three days later, one by one the puppies died, despite all her efforts and concern.

POST-PARTURITION PROBLEMS

A complaint that all knowledgeable breeders fear is fading puppy syndrome: if you have experienced it, the memory of it will live with you forever. We have had to deal with this, and the thought of it drives a knife through my heart to this day. The puppies are born healthy and of the correct weight and size, and in our case, all fed and appeared to thrive normally. The day after whelping, one lacked lustre to the coat and squealed a high-pitched noise, moving away from mum and siblings; we tried to get the puppy to suckle, but to no avail. The vet was called and antibiotics were administered; we fed a hydrating fluid, given by the vet, but the puppy died. This pattern progressed with each puppy over a period of two days, and we lost the whole litter. To see perfectly healthy youngsters die without being able to do anything was terrible: we were shattered, the mother distraught.

We have never had this happen again. The same bitch went on to have subsequent litters with healthy puppies.

It is not always the case that all the puppies die, and there appears to be no scientific solution to this condition. Lots of theories abound but are not proven.

COMPLETION OF PARTURITION

So the litter is safely born, and mother and puppies are settled and doing well. Each breed will have its own idiosyncrasies, and you should know how proficient the dam of your breed is at looking after her babies. Some breeders feel the need to sleep in the room with the litter for a few nights, just to make sure the mother is careful and does not lie on puppies when she gets up to adjust her position. Other breeders know that the particular bitch can be safely left after the first night. If one thinks about it, nature deems that survival is necessary and instils care into the bitch. The other side is, as my farmer father used to say, 'If it's worth ought it is more likely to get run over!' The fact that we are orchestrating the future of our breed makes it a little more venerable.

The bitch will have a dark, but not offensive discharge for the first few days after parturition, which will turn clear red blood and may last for three or four weeks. Only seek veterinary attention if the discharge becomes foul-smelling.

Often two days after delivery the bitch will start scratching up her bed and digging, rather like she did in the first stages of labour: this is normal and due to after pains. It is advisable to discourage her from this practice, as puppies might get caught under the bedding and she could subsequently lie on one. It can be annoying, but she will quickly stop.

For at least the first week you will find that you spend your time counting puppies, even in your sleep! However, watching puppies grow and sleep, and wondering if they will develop as you want, is very satisfying.

9 THE FIRST EIGHT WEEKS

COMMON POST-NATAL CONCERNS

So whelping is complete and the mother is settled in the whelping box on clean bedding, the puppies are dry and tummies are filling as they suck; the mother will start to come into full milk production, the more the puppies suck. This is a rewarding sight, but the new family must still be carefully observed.

Some breeders will look at each puppy whilst it is still wet, when the bone structure can be assessed: the experienced eye can see shoulder placement, length of rib, hind angulations and the like. Once the puppy is dry and starts to fill out, these points are lost for the first couple of weeks.

At this stage the puppy resembles a slug: he is blind and deaf, and moves about by gripping the bedding with his forelegs, dragging his body behind him. He is entirely dependent on his dam for all his needs and protection, and her protective instinct will therefore be heightened – so respect her space, and don't allow children to dash around screaming, for example, but keep her immediate environment calm and peaceful.

Be vigilant that all the puppies obtain the dam's first milk, the colostrum; this is produced in the first twenty-four hours, and contains essential antibodies that will protect the new babies from infection during those first important four weeks of life when they are helpless.

Weigh each puppy regularly in order to gauge its growth rate. Keep a whelping notebook for each bitch, with records of how she performed during whelping, any problems, litter size, development of the puppies, their weight, how soon they took solids, and so on. This is a useful log to refer to, although each pregnancy could be different.

If the puppies are uneven in size, keep putting the smaller one on a teat so it has a chance to catch up with its littermates. In the author's opinion hand feeding should be a last resort, so don't panic and step in too soon, as this could mean that the puppy does not suck hard enough from the mother, and she will therefore cease to lactate as heavily. Mother's milk is always best.

Coping with Rejection

Very occasionally a bitch will reject her puppies. The squeaking little bundles can alarm a maiden bitch following whelping, and she is not sure what to do with them. Be kind but assertive: she must be put in the whelping box and restrained calmly, all the while reassuring her. Let the puppies suckle: this will start to relax her. She will settle after a while, and by the following day you will wonder what you were concerned about.

In some breeds or circumstances the bitch may reject her puppies completely,

HAND REARING

Occasionally hand rearing is necessary, however we have never hand fed successfully in the thirty-seven years we have bred dogs. If you keep attaching a puppy to the teat, it will eventually learn what to do.

Hand rearing a puppy is required if the bitch becomes ill or dies – which is highly unlikely – but it must be done with extreme care. If milk is administered too quickly, there is a risk that it will enter the lungs, which would lead to choking and pneumonia, invariably resulting in death in a puppy so young.

When supplementing a puppy, you should be aware of the correct milk to use. Puppies grow at a rapid rate and bitch milk is high in calories and twice as rich in fat, calcium, phosphorous and protein as goat's or cow's milk – so despite what many people think, these are not sufficient as a substitute milk for a puppy. Neither is milk substitute designed for the human baby, as the human baby has a slower growth rate.

Bitch milk replacement can be obtained from your vet or from some agricultural suppliers; even some dog food manufacturers now produce bitch replacement milk. This is usually bought in powder form, and the mixing instructions should be strictly followed: any deviation will not be good for the puppy and digestive problems could follow, affecting its development and possibly leading to its demise. So don't be tempted to add a little extra powder in the hope of making it grow more quickly. The temperature of the milk should be 38°C (100.4°F): too cold and it will reduce the puppy's body temperature, too hot and it could burn the puppy's mouth and cause hair loss.

One way of administering the milk is by syringe, just a few drops at a time, on the puppy's tongue; when it has swallowed, repeat the process – it will soon get the idea and wait for the milk. Alternatively a puppy feeding bottle with a teat could be used, which is closer to the way it would feed from its mother.

Only someone very experienced and confident should consider using an intra-gastric tube, as this is inserted directly into the stomach.

Whichever way a puppy is hand fed, it should be held with the hand supporting it with its head up, or if it is in the whelping box its head should be supported so that when milk is administered it slips down its throat. Never hold the puppy upside down as it could choke.

Initially the puppy should be fed little and often, every two to three hours, day and night, so help may be required and a rota put in place so that you can remain alert to its needs.

If supplementary care is required because the puppy has been orphaned, it is important that it is cleaned after each meal. The face and eyes should be cleaned with cotton wool dipped in clean, aired, boiled water, and the genitals must be gently rubbed so that the puppy will pass urine and faeces. Puppies do not perform these functions spontaneously.

Puppies should be kept at a constant temperature, which can be more difficult when they don't have a mother to snuggle up to. It is a wise thought to provide a heat pad in conjunction with the heat lamp or radiator, as this gives orphan puppies a feeling of support – but be aware that too much heat can have the same devastating effects as too little, so put the heat pad to one end so that the puppies can move away from the heat if necessary.

Hand rearing is time consuming and arduous, but to see puppies grow, thrive and become strong and active is a just reward for all the effort.

and will not nurture them and may even try to kill them. This would be a very extreme case. However, if this did happen, the puppies would need to be removed from the dam before she caused them any traumatic or even fatal injury.

A bitch with these severe traits should not be bred from, as quite clearly she has issues of temperament.

POSTNATAL HEALTH CONCERNS

Metritis

Metritis is an infection of the uterus and possibly also of the birth canal, often due to retained matter, perhaps afterbirth or a dead puppy. As the condition takes hold the bitch will lose interest in her puppies, become depressed, and develop a raised temperature, accompanied by a foul-smelling discharge.

These signs are generally easy to spot, so be vigilant, as the vet should be consulted quickly. If left unnoticed the bitch can lose her milk completely and may even die. With antibiotics, she should recover with no ill-effect.

Some breeders will have the vet administer Oxytocin as a matter of course when a bitch has finished whelping, just to guard against these problems. However, Oxytocin makes the uterus contract, and if the bitch has finished whelping the uterus is already contracted, so the effect of administering Oxytocin can be detrimental to the uterus. So you have to make an informed choice.

The bitch will probably have a discharge for quite a while after whelping. It will probably be discoloured to start with, and will turn to red watery blood after a couple of days. This is normal, providing the discharge is not foul smelling. Sometimes the uterus fails to return to its normal size, initially – known as placental subinvolution – and this can be the cause; however, it will right itself in time. Just change the bedding often so as to keep the area clean.

Mastitis

Mastitis is an infection of the milk gland, due to the gland not being sucked out. This could be for various reasons: the

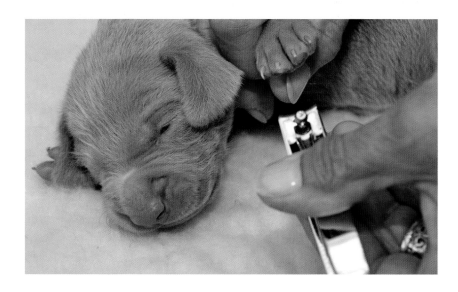

Puppies' nails should be cut regularly to avoid scratching mum.

teat may be too big or too small for the puppy to latch on to; if the puppies' nails are not cut regularly they are extremely sharp, and as they pummel the mother's mammary glands their nails will scratch her, making her sore, and therefore unlikely to let them keep on suckling.

The milk gland of the teat becomes swollen, hard and very warm to the touch; it will be painful and can make the bitch uncomfortable. If detected early enough, drawing the milk out of the teat can alleviate the symptoms, along with a cold pad on the gland. If this does not bring relief, veterinary interaction should be sought and antibiotics given.

The reason each puppy always sucks from the same teat is because in a small litter the unused teats will dry up naturally, thereby avoiding the risk of mastitis. Nature is so clever!

As the puppies become older and stronger mastitis tends not to occur because normally they would suck out the bitch very well.

Whenever you are pass the whelping box, or the mother is out to stretch her legs, just feel all her teats on a regular basis, to check that all is well. Prevention is better than cure!

Eclampsia or Milk Fever
Milk fever is generally more likely to occur in a bitch producing a lot of milk, often due to a large litter, and it arises because calcium is drained too quickly from her system. Symptoms could be that she is stiff and inactive when asked to come out for a walk. She could also be over-excited and restless. Usually the first course of action is to administer calcium intravenously, which will get the calcium straight into the bloodstream and consequently working quickly.

It is wise to follow this up with a supplement, usually added to the bitch's food, consisting of calcium, phosphorous and Vitamin D. This can be obtained from any good pet food and requisite supplier, as it is sold as a branded product. Alternatively your vet will be able to supply you with these products. Again, vigilance and speed of treatment is of the essence in order for the treatment to be successful.

CONGENITAL OR GENETIC PROBLEMS
Problems of this description are usually noticeable when the puppy is new born; symptoms are often presented within the first week of age.

Infection of the Umbilical Cord
Infection can occur if the umbilical cord is cut with a dirty instrument; alternatively sometimes too clean and sharp a cut means that infection can enter easily, particularly if the bedding is not cleaned thoroughly before being used for the whelping. The area should be bathed with clean cotton wool dipped in warm, previously boiled water with some salt dissolved in it. Salt is a fantastic antiseptic and healing component for many conditions.

If infection takes hold, the vet must be called and antibiotics prescribed, otherwise the infection could lead to joint ill. Joint ill is a serious condition where the infection goes straight into the system of the young animal, often through the umbilical opening, and will cause inflammation, swelling and pain of the joints; it can cause death. It is, however, very rare in dogs.

In normal circumstances the umbilical cord will dry and shrivel up within a day, which in turn seals the opening.

Hernias

Umbilical hernia: A protrusion from the umbilical ring, which has not closed properly, sometimes from the bitch being overzealous when cutting the cord, or from a hereditary cause. If the soft swelling is small it will probably disappear with no ill effects.

If the protuberance is bigger than the size of a large grape, it may require surgical assistance. Most vets would want to wait until the puppy is over twelve weeks of age before administering anaesthetic, unless the puppy's wellbeing were at risk, therefore you would need to inform the buyer of the puppy of the condition and adjust costs accordingly. Once the hernia has been repaired the dog should lead a totally normal existence. However, it is advisable that the dog is not used for breeding.

Inguinal hernia: Generally hereditary. Inguinal hernia appears as a swelling in the groin; the opening is in the inguinal canal. In the male puppy, this could prevent the testicles descending; in a bitch it may affect the uterus in adulthood, so will necessitate an operation.

Cleft Palate

As with humans, a cleft palate is often seen in conjunction with a hair lip. It is often a hereditary condition. In mild cases the dog can lead a long healthy life; however, more often the puppy will have to be put to sleep because the cavity in the roof of the mouth causes nutrition to be expelled through the nose, and so the puppy will not thrive. The condition is more prevalent in short-nosed breeds.

If this condition is thought to be hereditary, obviously the bitch should not be bred from.

Open Fontanelle

This is a rare condition that mainly affects breeds such as Chihuahuas, due to their apple-shaped skull. Because the skull retains an opening gap instead of the two parts fusing together, the affected puppy could easily sustain brain damage; it should therefore be culled.

Jaw Problems

A puppy's mouth should be checked from the age of three to four weeks onwards, when those sharp teeth start to come through. A severe deformity of the bone structure of the mouth will be evident before this, and should be dealt with according to how and if the condition will affect the puppy in the future.

An overshot mouth is when the top jaw protrudes well over the scissor bite required by most breeds. This is considered a fault, and would affect the showing career of a puppy, even though it will be able to lead a normal life. If this imperfection is exaggerated and the top jaw protrudes greatly, it is called 'parrot mouth'. Again, this conformation obviously does not cause debility as we have had dogs in our boarding kennels with a parrot mouth, and they were fit, healthy and carrying weight. However, such dogs should not be bred from as these faults will be able to come through.

An undershot jaw is when the lower jaw protrudes well forwards from the revise scissor bite required by some breeds – for example the French Bulldog, the Lhasa Apso, and mainly these brachycephalic breeds, where the skull is relatively broad and short, the breadth being about 80 per cent of the length. ('Brachycephalic' comes from the Greek *brachy* meaning 'short', and *cephalic* meaning 'head'.)

Sometimes the bite will appear perfect at eight weeks of age, with big, white, well-positioned teeth. At four months when the teeth change from milk teeth to permanent teeth they can still develop correctly – and then at a year of age the mouth goes wrong, usually becoming undershot. This is a frustrating turn of events when the puppy's potential is taking shape, and would restrict its chance of winning in the show ring because this is generally a hereditary condition and it would be strictly penalized. If dogs with any known genetic faults are bred from, the breed will deteriorate, as would the puppy's breed if it were knowingly bred from with this condition

Hypoglycaemia

Hypoglycaemia is a metabolic condition usually found in puppies that have just been weaned, and is caused by worms, infection, and even vaccination. The puppy could have fits, be weak, disorientated and even collapse. It is possible to correct and prevent the condition by monitoring that the puppy is eating regularly, and in more intense situations by giving an ionizer-enriched drink. Toy breeds are most susceptible to this condition due to the fact that they have small livers and cannot store glucose and glycogen.

Cosmetic Malformations

Other malformations, which are generally cosmetic, are a twist in the tail. This can be caused by damage at, or just after, birth. This kink in the tail is regarded as a fault in most breeds, but is acceptable in Bulldogs. If the deformity is extensive it could relate to spina bifida. In coated breeds this is not noticeable unless it is felt, so it is worth checking from time to time.

PUPPY INFECTIONS

Sometimes a puppy has a swollen eye or eyes before the eyes are open. This can be caused by an infection coming out of the body in a place where it can be expelled or by conjunctivitis. Cooled, boiled salt water can be used to clean the affected eye frequently, and it will probably cause no problems once the eye is open.

Pyoderma
Impetigo

Impetigo is a mild form of pyoderma where the puppies develop unsightly, pus-filled spots; it is caught if the area where the puppies live is dirty. Cleaning with tea tree wipes or some other antibacterial agent can be effective. It is essential that the puppy bedding and whelping box is kept clean as a preventative. Keeping the puppies' nails short stops them scratching each other, and introducing infection.

Juvenile Cellulitis or Puppy Strangles

Juvenile cellulitis is a more severe form of puppy pyoderma, which if not detected and treated early can result in death. It starts with pimples around the eyes and muzzle. Pustules that develop inside the ears are an early sign of this distressing condition.

The pustules fill the ears, both inside and on the earflaps, and they weep profusely. In fact the whole head tends to swell as a result of the muzzle and lymph nodes swelling, particularly in the throat. If the throat swells excessively it can obstruct breathing and swallowing – hence the name 'puppy strangles'.

This is primarily an immune system disorder, but it can be caused by infection entering the system via a cut. This condition will not respond to antibiotic treatment alone, and will require steroid injections.

RIGHT: This puppy scratched his face on a plant in the owner's garden, and just two days later his face was badly swollen. This photograph was not taken at the height of the condition. It was not thought that the puppy would survive.

BELOW: This is the same puppy at one year of age, now perfectly happy and healthy.

It is most likely to occur in a puppy of about two to four months, and can take up to eight weeks to run its course. If the puppy is treated swiftly he can fully recover, but he may never grow hair back around the ears, eyes and muzzle.

THE FIRST EIGHT WEEKS

Week One

Puppies settle into a routine of eating and sleeping. At this stage they are born with the basic senses of touch, taste and smell; they feel cold and warmth as well as pain and hunger, and although they cannot see and hear at this stage, they are born with a strong instinct of eat or die, so can find a teat, once they start to gain strength at a day or so old.

Their coat should be shiny, and their belly full. The coat resembles waves, probably due to the time spent suspended in fluid. In Weimaraners this is very obvious due to the colour reflecting the light, and the colour of the coat gives the impression of distinct stripes. These disappear after a few days, but it is an interesting sight nonetheless.

Latched on to a teat the puppies have strong suction powers, and a strong thriving puppy will arch his neck and pummel the mammary glands each side of 'his'

The coat of the newborn Weimaraner puppy shows a distinct striped appearance.

teat to stimulate the milk to come down. If laid on fleece-type bedding he can grip easily, and the hind legs will push to support the effort.

Puppies will take a lot out of the mother, especially a big litter. The bitch should be fed with a good quality diet at least twice a day, depending on how she looks and how much milk she is giving to her puppies. As examples, we had one bitch that loved her puppies and was meticulous in her care of them, but just got fatter and did not make more milk than was necessary. Another became extremely thin because everything she ate went into her milk production; she therefore required an enormous amount of food just to keep body and soul

together. Both litters thrived well, however we introduced weaning at an earlier age with the litter that did not have the quantity of milk from the mother.

At three to four days old the dew claws can be removed. Some breeds are required to retain the dew claw and must have them on the hind pastern, but mostly they are better removed so as not to get caught on things when the dog is dashing around. The dew claw is basically the thumb, and in the majority of breeds is obsolete to requirements.

To remove they are simply cut off swiftly with curved scissors, and the puppy in fact makes more noise being picked up and taken away from mum,

REGISTERING A PUPPY WITH THE KENNEL CLUB

You will need a form from the Kennel Club, signed by the stud dog owner, and must then put down your names of choice. Make sure when filling in the part on colour, that the colour you register is recognized for the breed in question. Alternatively you can now register your litter online. If this is your preference, a letter will be sent to the stud dog owner making sure this was the dog you used.

The affix is explained in Chapter 1. How do you decide what name to have for your affix? Many people use an anagram of their own names or that of the first dog they owned. You have to submit to the Kennel Club alternative choices, as there are so many affixes registered that your first choice may be too near in interpretation to one that has already been granted to somebody else.

Our first choice was Roebuck, after the name of the lane we lived down at the time. Our second choice, Gunalt, came about because we had gundogs and the 'alt' flowed on nicely. We thought it short, easy to remember and pronounceable. How glad we were to have our second choice granted. The full name of a puppy (including the affix) cannot be more than twenty-four letters, so an affix that is short gives more choices of name.

Initials cannot be used, and nor can numbers, except in a name such as 'Silver Dancer the Second'. Canine terms such as 'Crufts' or 'bitch' are not permissible.

If no name is submitted, Kennel Club staff will decide on the name and a charge will be added.

Endorsements can be added to the registration of a puppy, such as 'Progeny not eligible for registration' or 'Not eligible for the issue of an Export Pedigree'.

Some breeders automatically add endorsements, which they are happy to remove if the new owner justifies the reason for removal. An endorsement may be added to a puppy that is not the quality to be bred from but can still live a fulfilling life and give enjoyment. The new owner should be informed of any endorsements on their new puppy, and written and signed conformation of this should be obtained from the new owner.

than when the procedure is being performed, as long as it is executed by an experienced person. Potassium permanganate crystals dipped in damp cotton wool will seal the cut and sanitize the minor wound.

At the same time one would arrange for the vet to dock the puppies' tails if it were legal and were felt necessary. Docking was effectively banned on 6 April 2007 in this country, but it has been banned for a number of years previously in most of Europe, Scandinavia and many countries throughout the world. Docking is legal if the owner of the litter has a gun licence and will be using the dog for gun work. However, it is illegal to take a docked dog born after this date into an environment where the public pay to attend, be it a dog show or game fair. To my mind this is quite bizarre, but as they say, 'Ours is not to reason why'!

After a few days, just to make sure all is well with the puppies, you can think about registering the litter with the Kennel Club; or you could become an accredited breeder and adhere to the rules laid down (*see* Chapter 1). To be honest, if you are breeding for the good of the breed you will want to do everything constructive for it, and as a result your dogs should meet the KC criteria, so why not go for accreditation? This will also give you a measure of safeguard in this society where people will 'sue for anything.'

If you prefer you can just register your litter.

Week Two

Even brand new puppies twitch and mumble in their sleep; I often wonder what they dream of. At two weeks they are getting stronger and in sleep will curl the lip and make small growling noises.

At around ten days of age the eyes start to open. Interestingly, bitches seem to open their eyes before dogs, but then girls are generally nosier than boys! Although it takes a little time for the eyes

At two weeks of age the puppy's eyes start to open.

At three weeks old the puppy can focus clearly and the ear placement starts to show.

to focus properly, as they open the puppies' heads are up, surveying their surroundings.

If bedding is the fleece type, they start to get up on their legs and wobble around, rather like a baby taking its first tentative steps. They are now showing more interest in their surroundings, rather than just eating and sleeping.

It is a good idea to advertise the puppies at this time. This gives you plenty of time to educate the prospective new owners on the idiosyncrasies of your particular breed. Having the litter sold early also removes the stress of wondering if you will be able to sell them all, consequently you will have the luxury of vetting homes more vigilantly and not just wanting them to go. It also gives new owners the opportunity to visit the litter and take photos, thus making documented facts to treasure of their puppy's start in life.

Week Three

At three weeks of age the sound of your voice will be interesting them, as from this time on, their neurological and physical advancement is rapid. They are starting to play with each other, and become alert when the mother returns to the nest. Purebred puppies start showing breed features in play even from this early stage, which is a source of great charm. They will now begin to give a modest bark, a great cause of amusement.

The puppies' worming programme can start at this time (*see* worming cycles on

Puppies quickly learn to associate the bowl with survival and eat heartily.

pages 178–9). In the author's opinion it is advisable to obtain worming preparations from the vet.

The puppies will now have the ability to lap, so towards the end of the third week, when the mother is away from them, you could try them with some pre-soaked, mashed-up puppy food, presented in a loose form. Pop the muzzle of the puppy into the dish, so that it gets a taste of the food. Initially the puppies will have more food on them than inside them, because they stand in the food and lick each other. However, let the mother back in with them and she will clean them up and finish the food they have left.

The bitch will probably come out to eat, but will then want to be straight back with the puppies so that she can regurgitate her dinner for them to eat. This is Nature's way of weaning.

Weeks Four and Five
Now the puppies know that when they hear your voice, you will be bringing food. Their mentality at this age is survival, so food is their motivation. As they reach the five week period, upon the sound of the door they are out of the box and waiting for the bowl to be placed down for them to eat.

The puppies will be fed four times a day at this stage. We feed a propriety complete food, still soaked for one meal and fed dry at others, to give variety and introduce the crunch: this will ultimately be how the puppy is fed. Feeding food dry helps keep dentition in order and teeth clean. It is also hygienic, as food does not turn sour if left down for any period, and disposal of such food would encourage vermin.

Fresh water must be available at all times for the puppies, so as to prevent dehydration.

Some breeders swear by fresh meat and biscuits, but truly this is personal preference. However, pet food manufactures are part of a multi-million-pound industry. Research into feeding dogs is extensive, so when a food is called 'complete', that is what you get. Feeding 'fresh scraped meat, wholemeal biscuits, cream and sardines for the oil' sounds romantic, but it is not balanced, and does not contain the nutrients, trace elements, vitamins, etc. required for a balanced diet.

Each breed will need an individual way of feeding amounts, applicable to their needs. Some breeds can eat an unlimited amount and not become overweight due to their activity levels and growth rates. Other breeds just look at food and put on weight. It is advisable to speak with experienced people within your chosen breed.

Remember to keep cutting the white tip off the nails, otherwise they will seriously scratch the mother. As the teeth are coming through and are as sharp as needles, they can cause the bitch considerable pain pulling at the teats, so she may not want to stay with them all the time.

We keep the litter in a puppy unit, in a kennel, and the mother is allowed out regularly. At this age the puppies can get out of the whelping box, so we go into the kennel often and wake them up, then lift them out of the box. As they have just awakened they will want to pass urine, so will do this out of the box. Very quickly, within a couple of days, they learn this pattern, hence keeping the sleeping area clean and dry.

We would then remove the fleece bedding (which is likely to block the washing machine when impregnated with shavings), giving instead clean white shredded paper in the whelping box, and wood shavings in the playing area. The reason we use shavings probably stems from our farming roots. We reared baby pigs on shavings, as they smell clean and absorb any fouling, leaving the young animals clean and sweet-smelling. When the shavings are dirty they are easily

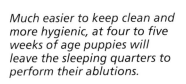

Much easier to keep clean and more hygienic, at four to five weeks of age puppies will leave the sleeping quarters to perform their ablutions.

removed with a hand shovel and bucket, and just as easily disposed of.

Newspaper will not have the same effect, and is time consuming: even if one is diligent in trying to keep things clean, the faeces will sit on the paper, so puppies are constantly walking and rolling about in them.

Week Six
Puppies are self-assured at this age, and will be feeding heartily from the food you supply.

The dam can be weaned off them at this age, although no hard and fast rules apply. Some bitches like to go in and see their puppies, but rush straight out as soon as those needle teeth fasten on their teats; others are happy to feed the puppies for longer. If the mother's milk has been supplemented with milk substitute whilst she was feeding her babies, now is the time to cut this out, thus enabling her milk supply to diminish. Increase her exercise to help get her back into condition, and worm both mother and puppies.

The puppies should be given toys and plenty of stimulation. Initially, discarded household and toilet paper cardboard rolls are a great source of fun. The puppies will be more involved with each other than playing with you.

Avoid giving small balls to large breeds as these could become caught in the back of the throat and cut off the air supply. Also toys connected to ropes, as the rope could get wrapped round a puppy's neck causing strangulation.

Make sure that enough toys are given out so that the puppies are not quarrelling over them.

Week Seven
Now the puppies' perspective changes. Instead of 'eat or die' they are more interested in interacting with you when you take the food to them. If the weather is clement the puppies can come out and play on the lawn, and then you will see the 'pack' element of their temperament developing. Hierarchy will be visible and individual characters present.

This is the time when the puppy can be chosen to suit the new owner. It is enthralling, watching the different ways in which each puppy's traits are manifested. I have not previously mentioned marking for identification, for this reason. (As a breeder, you will know how to differentiate between puppies when younger, simply by living with them.)

Each puppy will try to monopolize your attention, which only goes to show that they will soon need to leave their siblings and have the individual attention that a new residence will give them. They are serious time wasters.

Watching puppies go about their business you may find that you will often be drawn to one puppy. Looking at that puppy will give a guide as to whether he will develop as a dog with show potential, and consequently a dog to be bred on from. Breeders will often stack a puppy in a show pose, to see if he is balanced and full of type.

This is an art, but great fun, too. It is also a useful way of giving a puppy human contact, and it shows him that you are the 'boss' or pack leader: what you say must be adhered to.

Week Eight
How can you part with them? Believe me, with the amount they eat, the amount they deposit and the amount of noise they make – easily! Seriously, at eight weeks a puppy is mentally ready to learn more on a one-to-one level: he needs

ABOVE: At seven weeks of age, inquisitive minds will be stimulated with play and differing environments. In temperate weather puppies love exploring the garden.

BELOW: The breeder evaluates the puppy's potential.

human interaction, stimulation and company. You cannot successfully give eight-week-old puppies what they need in mental terms, and if they are going to knowledgeable, well-prepared homes, as they all should be, you should be happy to see them go.

Now is the time for some serious viewing of the puppies by their prospective new owners, and the time they will leave to go to their new home. The litter should have been advertised earlier, and hopefully new owners will be waiting. It is an object lesson in psychology, making sure that each owner is happy in the

To fulfil a dog's mental and physical development sufficiently, he requires one to one interaction. This development is displayed perfectly in this champion Pointer.

thought that they are taking away the best puppy.

Breeders who have built a good reputation of producing quality dogs from a recognized line will have a list of owners waiting and may not need to take a deposit. We would rather someone had the facility to change their mind at the last minute, than take a puppy just because they would lose the deposit. On the other hand, if you are just starting out it is a different thing and you would be wise to take a deposit, just to make sure your buyer is serious.

We have a saying, 'A puppy is not sold until he is paid for and leaves for his new home.' It is easy for a potential buyer to get excited when seeing new puppies, but a whole different thing when it comes to taking one home. When owners come to collect, advise them to bring a towel to put on their knee for the journey home. The puppy will probably never have been in a car and may suffer travel sickness. Whilst dogs travelling in cars are safer in a crate in the back, the first journey is bound to be stressful, and cuddling him on your knee is kinder, just this once.

When all puppies have left the premises, it is important that the whelping kennel is washed thoroughly, followed by steam cleaning. This should be done again the week before the kennel is to be used for another whelping. Always have a separate kennel that is used only for whelping, to stop the spread of disease.

It is not usual for a bitch to pine for her puppies when they have left, as she has generally finished with them by then. Nevertheless if a puppy is retained she will take care of it, but will also not hesitate to scold it if it steps out of line.

As the puppy grows, mother and puppy become quite independent of one another in time.

10 FINDING SOUND HOMES

ADVERTISING THE LITTER

Finding sound homes is of great importance, and I would recommend that advertising the litter is started early, when you are sure that all the puppies are thriving. When the puppies are about a week old is probably the best time to place your advert. If you have a website, you can inform 'surfers of your site' that a particular bitch has been mated, to which sire, and the date that she is due.

Leaving the advertising too late can mean that you are left with puppies, as people are not as keen to take a wild twelve-week-old puppy! They would always rather have it as a smaller bundle, at the usual eight weeks of age. Some 'breeders' are of the ethos that if they can't sell the puppies they will just keep them all! This is not only a foolhardy philosophy, but positively cruel to the puppies, since it is impossible for one family or person to give each puppy from a whole litter the mental and physical attention it needs. The puppies would inevitably end up feral.

Other breeders panic when they are left with a bunch of ten- to twelve-week-old puppies eating them out of house and home and making a mess everywhere, so they sell the puppies to 'pet supermarkets' or dealers.

Either option is certainly not to be recommended.

Using the Internet

There is a growing trend to advertise puppies on the internet. The internet is certainly very useful for letting people know you exist and for initial inquiries, and it is great for websites and the many other ways of communicating and learning about breeds and where to find

Mike Gadsby and Jason Lynn are renowned for producing quality, as this American Cocker Spaniel shows. (Photo: Jason Lynn)

reputable breeders; the Kennel Club is a good example. My reservation is that buyers are sometimes drawn to advertising pages that do not check the breeders, or the claims made by some breeders. Consequently, conscientious breeders are classed alongside those who are perhaps not as scrupulous, and who therefore give all dog breeders a bad name. So before advertising in this format, check the host site carefully.

The Kennel Club gives guidance on where to buy a puppy. Accredited breeders are given priority (another reason to join the scheme), but all puppies registered can go on a list given out by the KC to potential buyers. However, if you are advertising through newspapers and journals, pick reputable ones, and as previously stated, start advertising early. This gives you the chance to weed out unsuitable potential buyers. Advertising is expensive, but trying to do it 'on the cheap' could work out to be a false economy if people looking for a puppy can't find the advertisement.

Word of Mouth

As you become established as a breeder, you will find that word of mouth and reputation become an invaluable way of finding fitting homes for your puppies. Most top breeders have waiting lists of 'vetted' people who are quite happy to wait for the right puppy, from the right breeder. Equally, prospective owners who are intelligent and forward thinking will have done their research and found the established breeders with the good reputation, so why would they buy from anyone else? They are much more likely to go on a waiting list to have the puppy from the breeder they feel confident in.

A novice breeder who is just starting out and has not yet built a reputation is going to find it harder to weed out the time wasters.

Taking a Deposit

If a prospective buyer meets with your approval and puts his name down to reserve a puppy, both parties often feel more confident in the proposed transaction if a deposit is left as security of their intentions. The amount of money put down should be agreeable to both parties; this is generally about 15 per cent of the price of the puppy, and is not returnable if the prospective owner changes their mind. In principle it gives the breeder confidence that the buyer is serious, and he can keep a count of how many puppies are in fact sold.

Of course there are also those who enquire about a puppy and say they want one, but then omit to tell the breeder they have gone elsewhere or changed their mind.

We don't take any deposit because we would rather the prospective owner had the chance to change their mind about having a puppy if the timing wasn't right for them, or if they got 'cold feet' about the prospect of puppy ownership. We feel it is better to have the puppy stay with us initially, than to have it returned at a later stage because the foundation for taking it was not sound enough.

EDUCATING NEW OWNERS

Educating the new owner is a fundamental requirement for the wellbeing and future happiness of your puppy. If you are a new breeder and have possibly only owned a bitch before, this will prove difficult *unless you research your breed well*. There are several pointers you might bear in mind in the course of this research. First, it is always useful to glean

REHOMING RESPONSIBILITIES

If you are going to breed dogs, you should be accountable for the puppies produced. If puppies were always bred and homed conscientiously, there would be little need for rehoming establishments.

It is your responsibility to take back a dog bred by you, if the home does not work out satisfactorily. It is often the case that the owner has indulged the dog as a puppy. By the time it grows into an adolescent it thinks it is higher in the pecking order than some members of the family. The scenario may be such that the dog growls at the human or his family, the human starts to feel insecure with the dog – and so the dog is returned to the breeder.

It is extremely hard to find a home for a dog in this instance, but the alternative is devastating – which is why the support and education of potential owners is essential.

Each purebred breed of dog has its own independent rescue service, a charitable organization run by volunteers. If you have trouble rehoming a returned dog they will endeavour to help – but be prepared to make a donation.

Trained properly, large dogs like these are not a threat to children.

information from skilled breeders to learn the pertinent features of their breed. In particular, large, strong-willed breeds will require great depth of knowledge; in these breeds, dogs tend to be dominant in their thinking and could be harder to understand. Small breeds, on the other hand, may become indulged, bringing their own problems.

It is essential that you are always available when new owners need advice and guidance.

We might go back to the analogy with buying a car: if you wish to buy a family car with confidence you would go to a dealership that specializes in the make of car you are interested in. If, on the other hand, you just want any old car, you might go to a back-street trader who could sell you a dud; at best when a prob-

lem arises with the car and you need the fault correcting, you return to the trader only to find him gone. At worst, a more serious problem with the car puts your family at risk. The same scenario could well occur with dog breeders.

The psychology of how a dog might think in relation to his new owner is discussed in the next chapter.

Choosing a Puppy

The potential for owners to choose a puppy by markings or colour can be an issue. A puppy should be chosen on the suitability of its disposition to fit the needs of the family. If puppies are booked at birth or advertised early, potential owners can come and visit the litter often, particularly if they live in the vicinity. We are always happy for excited

From an early age, puppies' instincts will become apparent.

owners to visit and take photos of the developing litter.

The new owner will often alight on a particular puppy, especially if it is easy to pick out because of its colour or markings. This should be discouraged, because a puppy's character, and how well it can be anticipated to fit in with the family's needs, is much more important. For instance, if the puppy is a gundog breed, is he to be worked in the field? If he is, then the puppy selected should be the one that always has his nose to the ground, scouting around, off looking for 'game', and if a toy or knotted sock is

thrown within his sight he should be off after it, anxious to retrieve it.

The theory that one should not go for the individual that appears shy because it is often sitting in the corner really does not apply: for the experienced breeder, breeding puppies of uniformly good temperament is paramount, and often the quiet one is the thinking puppy – his temperament is perfectly reliable, he just prefers not to rush about aimlessly.

Building a relationship with your puppy buyers is important. If confidence in you is established, the owner will feel secure in your guidance.

Some new owners are anxious that the breeder will not be able to recognize the puppy they have selected, and to differentiate them, collars of different colours can be put on the puppies. We will not do this, however, for fear that the collar could get caught on something and risk strangling the puppy. Besides, the dedicated breeder will have watched the puppies closely and can generally tell them apart easily, even if they are all the same colour. If this is not the case, it is much safer to clip a small piece of hair from the puppy; some breeders mark the puppy with a splodge of nail polish inside the ear.

Ultimately, puppy and owner will develop together, providing a stable foundation for all.

Preparing the Puppy for its New Home
The responsible breeder will advise new owners as to ways they can help the puppy settle in to its new home. For instance, when they visit before the puppy is due to go, they might bring with them a piece of bedding from the new home, which can be put in with the litter. When they finally take the puppy away, they take the piece of bedding too, so

that it smells of where the puppy came from and will afford him some reassurance in his strange new home.

Another somewhat old-fashioned idea is to put an alarm clock and a hot water bottle under the bedding: the regular tick and extra warmth are reassuring to the puppy, and may be effective in helping him to settle down.

It can take a few days for the puppy to settle in to his new surroundings. He has lived all his life in an environment that included his littermates, so the anxiety of change, solitude from other siblings, different germs and even water is bound to be upsetting; this can have a physical manifestation, too, in an upset tummy. This can last a few days, but if the puppy is happy in himself, obviously settling in and running around, avoid rushing to the vet for antibiotics, as this might add to the upset.

New owners who have little experience of a young puppy should note that when a puppy eats a big meal, he often shakes as he settles down after his food. This is quite normal.

THE PSYCHOLOGY OF OWNING A DOG

As a breeder it is essential that you understand how a dog thinks and reacts during various stages of his life, and you need to educate the new owner in this knowledge. The basic premise is that the

Whether large or small, all breeds of dogs have instincts, and therefore will need guidance from their owner.

ABOVE: A well-bred dog in a knowledgeable and loving home – the aim of a breeder.

BELOW: Taught with respect, dogs and children can become great pals, but remember never to leave them alone together unsupervised.

dog lives in a pack, and potential owners must be made aware that they must be pack leaders from the start. This does not involve cruelty, but a clear understanding of canine psychology.

Although their puppy is an animal, he is invariably treated as a member of the family. This is the reason that we have pet dogs: to gain companionship, pleasure and loyalty. A dog that grows up in the family alongside the children gives them a better understanding of the value of care and respect; it also teaches them to have compassion for animals, all valuable lessons for a child's future.

However, we, as humans, think in an entirely different way to the way a dog thinks. Even at a very young age individual views are formed, and to put a child into an environment where he or she must be totally subservient to their peers would stifle their mental development.

A dog, on the other hand, being a pack-oriented animal, needs to observe the pecking order in the pack hierarchy in order to live contentedly, and we should not try to change his instinct by humanizing him. Take, for example, the Toy Poodle that will not allow any one to sit on his chair and will only eat hand-cooked chicken or salmon: the poodle is not by nature a neurotic snappy dog, but if he is indulged and treated like a child he is made to feel insecure because he doesn't know where he fits into the pack hierarchy. This is why he snaps.

Consistency is needed with dogs. An adult or child should never tease a puppy, but if a higher member of the pack – in this case you – wants the toy or chew that he is enthralled with, he must realize that your acquisitive behaviour is quite acceptable. For example, when dogs are in a pack situation, a dog higher in the pecking order will approach, and stand over, a subordinate chewing a bone, and the underdog will back off, and the higher pack dog will take the bone. This is usually done when the underdog is in a vulnerable position – lying down, for instance – so avoiding confrontation and any chance of a fight. The dog that took the bone will walk away and then probably discard the bone – he didn't want it, he was just taking the opportunity to prove his position in the pack. The underdog did not object, because the psychology proved that, although he may be fitter, he was unlikely to win the battle on this occasion.

In similar small ways you can demonstrate to the puppy your position of supremacy in the family hierarchy. For example, when he is eating his meal, you might (very occasionally) pick up his bowl, just to confirm to him that you are 'boss'. Ask him to sit and wait patiently, then give the food back and let him go back to it on command. Another way to show your supremacy is always to walk through a door first: he should not be allowed to push past you, and if necessary restrain him – though be sure to praise him when he gets the message.

This is the way we should think – and avoid confrontation if at all possible.

Most problems with the grown dog – assuming they have been bred correctly – originate from uninformed early training: their owners have allowed them to develop bad habits because they, the owners, don't know any better. For example, the adult dog that dashes to the door and throws himself at the person entering has developed that trait because everyone who came into the home when he was a puppy fawned over him, and he still expects the same. So don't allow people to pet a puppy as they enter, and then he won't expect it, and don't allow him to rush to greet them and jump all over them – this might be amusing when he is a puppy, but certainly in a large breed, not when he is full grown. In the same way never make a game of retrieving the post, but make the puppy stay quiet whilst you accept the mail – then he will never learn to jump at the postman and potentially become aggressive towards him.

PAPERWORK FOR THE NEW OWNER

When a puppy is to be collected by a new owner it is efficient to have ready all documents relating to the puppy, as well as a supply of the food he is used to, and any requisites that are to accompany him.

He should therefore be sent away with a comprehensive diet sheet detailing what he has been fed at breakfast, lunch, tea/dinner and supper, and whether the food is soaked or fed dry. Stress on this sheet that clean fresh water is to be available at all times. It might also be suggested in this document at what age to reduce the number of meals given. In several breeds it is wise always to feed two meals a day. Point out if the breed of choice has any idiosyncrasies with regard to feeding.

The new owner may ultimately want to change the feeding system – everyone has differing ideas – however it is wise to send the puppy off with a supply of the brand of food he has been fed on when with you, the breeder, and to advise the new owner to feed this to the puppy at least for the first week. This will be one less stress for the puppy during this time of immense change in his life: the stress of change can lead to an upset tummy, so having the stability of the same food is

The folder containing the documents for the puppy.

important. This also gives the new owners time to obtain the right food for the new arrival.

As mentioned above, it is also a good idea to send the puppy off with a toy or a piece of blanket that smells of the litter.

All these things show that you are thoughtful and professional, and this will help to reassure the new owner, and to give them self-assurance.

It should also be documented how the puppy has been wormed, and when. The new owner can then inform his own vet, who can advise on a future worming regime.

In today's climate, it is wise to include a contract specifying warranty, disclaimer and conditions of sale, which both parties will sign. We took solicitors' advice on the wording of this document.

We include an information brochure within our puppy folder, giving basic advice on what to expect from the puppy – how he might be expected to settle in, the basic initial training he might be given, and potential problem areas. Although new owners will have been to see both the puppies and us on more than one occasion, they quickly forget the advice previously given: the excitement of having a new puppy makes it easy to forget things!

Included in this leaflet we list breed clubs and sponsorship forms, should the new owner be interested in becoming a member, along with useful books relating to the breed. We also reiterate essential equipment, such as an indoor kennel, fleece bedding, stainless steel bowls and recommended toys that won't cause damage to a puppy. We will also advise when and how to clean the puppy's ears if necessary, and when and how to cut the toe nails.

Insurance

Taking out a limited insurance policy very often gives the new owner peace of mind. Certain companies offer breeders four weeks free cover to send away with each puppy: the breeder simply sends by phone or email the details of each puppy, and the new owner's details, to the company, and the puppy is then allocated a number which can be used if a claim is required within those four weeks.

This gives owners more time to investigate insurance policies at their leisure, and thoroughly read the small print. The cheapest policy is not always the most cost effective: insurance is a costly item, but vets' fees can be massive, so it is not something to be rushed into.

The Kennel Club
Registration Form

The puppy's pedigree and the Kennel Club registration form are also necessary inclusions in the documents to go with the puppy. The registration form includes all the relevant details of the puppy: his registered name – as given by the breeder, but not necessarily the pet name chosen by the new owner – his breed, colour, sex, date of birth, and KC registration number, applicable only to him. It will also have details of his sire and dam, and any relevant health screening that the parents have had.

The breeder must sign the section on the back of the form, confirming that they are the present owner of the puppy. The new owner can then change the ownership of the puppy into their name.

Receipt

Having a receipt is obviously necessary from the purchaser's point of view, and from the seller's it is also useful, as they then have all the puppy's details, plus any specific conditions of sale and the date, safe in one book.

Receipt books are easily obtained from the publishers of some dog publications. This would take the form of a duplicate page, listing the name of the puppy, its breed, date of birth, sire, dam, new owner's details, price, and the date it was taken. As a result you have a copy of all the puppy buyers' details, which you can keep for future reference.

VACCINATIONS

Puppies have immunity from disease from antibodies that pass to them through the blood supply in the placenta, however this is only a small amount. Through their mother's milk they gain about 75 per cent immunity – except, of course, this is depleted when the puppies are weaned.

The initial injection the puppy receives covers canine distemper, hepatitis, leptospirosis, parainfluenza and parvovirus. This vaccine is administered by one injection, abbreviated to DHLPP. We now have the pet passport, too, which enables dogs to move freely throughout Europe. This means the recipient can also have a vaccine against rabies.

It is sometimes the case that the breeder has the first set of inoculations given to the puppies by his own vet before they leave to their new abode. However, we understand from our vet that this can be a useless exercise, as different vets use different brands of vaccine, so if the breeder's vet uses one company's vaccine and the future owner uses a different brand, the manufacturer will not take responsibility if the puppy develops a problem. It is therefore better that you consult your vet about vaccinations; he will be aware if there is a problem with illness in your region, so he is the person to advise as to when the puppy should be vaccinated.

Breeders should be mindful to promote relations with their vet, and not alienate him by implying that they know his job better than he does. Similarly the new owner would always be well advised to seek out a reputable vet, and a good way to start would be to take the puppy for a check-up soon after taking him home.

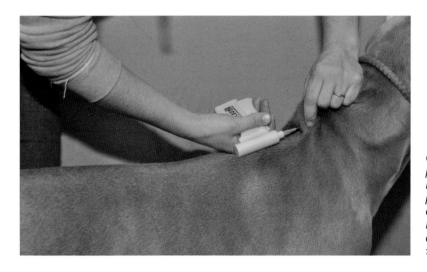

Chipping is a permanent way of identifying your pet. The chip is easily inserted with little or no discomfort to the dog.

A scanner simply reads the unique identifying number.

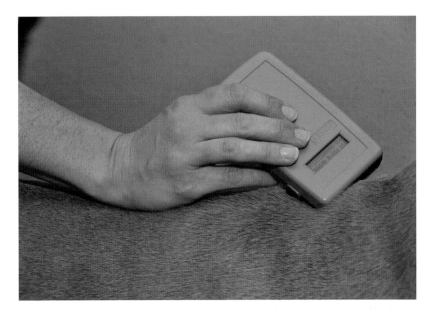

Off to a new home – the puppy leaves with his new owners.

This would also be a good time to discuss further worming, and the puppy can be microchipped at this time.

LEAVING HOME!

So all is now ready for the puppy to be taken to his new home: he is chosen and paid for, the relevant documents have been received by the new owner, a supply of puppy food (the brand he is familiar with, supplied by the breeder) has been put up to go with him, and any other requisites – toys, bedding – gathered together.

Probably the kindest way for the puppy to travel on this, his first journey, is on an old towel or puppy pad on his new owner's knee, and cuddled (the towel is in case he is sick or has an accident). He could be placed in the estate part of the car, preferably in a cage (for his own safety), but on this occasion he is going to feel stressed as he has no idea where he is going, and it is the first time he has been separated from his siblings. (On future journeys it is wise to get the puppy used to travelling in the back, as he will be much safer there.)

And so the breeder waves goodbye, knowing that the puppy he has invested so much care in producing is off to an educated, caring home.

I have often been asked if I am sad to see a puppy leaving with his new family, and the reply is always the same: 'NEVER!' If I have done my job correctly, he will get what we cannot give him: the individual attention he needs for his growth and development.

Transporting dogs is safer if the animal is secure in a crate.

11 GENERAL HEALTH AND PROBLEMS

HUSBANDRY OF THE OLDER DOG

Retiring the Brood Bitch

How do you decide when your brood bitch should finish with producing puppies? The guidelines would be that she has had two or more Caesarean sections, probably as a result of inertia or whelping-related problems. In some breeds, when normal whelping is not an option, you must ask yourself whether you should breed from a dog that is unable to self-whelp; if you are prepared to do this, again only you can take the responsibility of how many litters you will take from a bitch in these circumstances. The Kennel Club principles on breeding from a bitch are clearly set out: a maximum of six litters from one bitch, and she must not be over eight years of age at the last time of whelping (in exceptional circumstances application may be made to the Kennel Club before mating takes place, for their consideration).

Many breeders make the decision to have an older bitch that has finished her breeding programme spayed/neutered. The main reason for this is to prevent pyometra, a womb infection that often occurs in later life; this could require an emergency operation, and the risk to the health of the bitch would be much greater due to her advancing years. Besides, a spayed bitch does not come into season, making life more relaxed for all.

Homing the Retired Dog

If many dogs are kept, one option is to home an older bitch or dog with a family who are familiar with the breed and can give more individual attention to an older canine.

The down side to this is the guilt the breeder feels. Why is this? People are always quick to condemn such a decision, being of the vociferous opinion that 'that bitch (or dog) has served the breeder well and is discarded when of no further use to them!' However, if the breeder knows a home that would be pleased to have an older canine, why not let the older bitch have that quality of life perhaps not afforded to her in a pack situation, despite the fact that she is loved and well cared for with the breeder. We have let a retired brood bitch go to a known loving home, because we loved her enough!

The Old Dog in the Pack

Humans think they have the monopoly on civilized behaviour, yet it is enlightening to watch how the hierarchy works in a pack of dogs.

So how does an old dog maintain his level of authority in the pack? As a dog becomes older and loses his strength, he will still need to somehow prove his supremacy, and this is achieved by waiting until younger, fitter males are in a vulnerable position – for example, a young dog is lying down chewing on a bone, and the older dog goes and stands over the young dog, thereby placing himself psychologically in a strong position, a dominant pose. He will growl to demand the prize – the bone – and the young male, if he is wise, will identify that he cannot win over the situation, so gives up the bone to the older dog.

An older bitch will often snap determinedly at youngsters around her, fearful that in their rough play they might bump into her because she is no longer quick enough to avoid them as they dash about. But they learn to respect the old lady, and this unspoken respect is a joy to see. Our dogs all live together, and we find an older dog gains respect from the pack. If playing youngsters do inadvertently bump into an old one, he will snap at them crossly and the young ones dash off, duly scolded. They could easily have the upper hand, but they show the old one the reverence he deserves.

When someone behaves despicably, they are often said to be 'acting like an animal'. How erroneous this is, when animals generally have a very definite, mutually understood code of conduct that is based on respect!

As he gets older the dog, like us humans, often needs extra attention – and he likes a bit more comfort, such as another layer on the bed. His hearing begins to go, and perhaps his sight, too. He gets much slower in the way he moves around, and starts to lose mobility. Patience is needed then as his faculties diminish. We had an old bitch that often became alarmed if voices were raised, for whatever reason; because this was not the norm, she felt vulnerable and would panic, and we would have to restrain her and calm her.

Older dogs cope well with these changes, however, sensing how to con-

Older dogs need and deserve special comfort and care – they have served you well.

TIME TO LET GO

Breeds age at different times. With most of the large and/or heavy breeds the length of life tends to be much shorter, and eight or nine is considered old – though of course there is always the exception, and one hears of twenty-year-old dogs. Small and medium breeds can happily reach fifteen or more – and more of these do, nowadays, due to better nutrition and care. But whatever the age of your dog, when he dies, the heartbreak is immense. Nevertheless we must be honest about when it is time to say goodbye: sometimes we kid ourselves that our much loved pet is fine because he wags his tail or eats a little more today, when really he has lost his quality of life and it would be kinder to seek euthanasia.

This is such a hard option, because often the dog has been such an integral part of our lives, has been at our side through the birth of our children and other great milestones in our progress through life. But for the love of our companion we should ask ourselves if he still has the quality of life he deserves: is he distressed and in pain? Can he move freely? Can he perform his normal bodily functions? Is he eating and drinking to sustain preservation?

If any or all of these issues seriously affects him, one must truthfully assess his quality of life, because what we *can* do is grant him the kindness and dignity to put him out of his pain, despite our own heartache. Very often it takes a friend who does not see the dog each day to tell us when it is time to let go.

This is a positive thing we can do for our loved companion.

A Dangerous Dog

It should go without saying that any dog with an aggressive or nervous disposition should never be bred from, whatever the reasons for justifying this decision. And if a dog is overly aggressive, even proving dangerous, you should consider carefully his quality of life, as well as whether he is likely to bite someone. It may be difficult to envisage having a physically healthy dog put to sleep, but it is important to be realistic: no man is an island, and such a dog in these circumstances cannot be allowed to continue with life –the responsibility is too great.

When bred soundly and owned with support and knowledge, the dog will become his owner's best pal.

duct themselves in their normal sur-roundings. Problems tend only to arise if the layout of their environment is changed. Dogs also have the ability to adjust with age. They will often play enthusiastically, running about as best they can with a puppy or younger dog, but then will sleep longer, later!

Nutrition: the Senior Diet

Pet food manufacturers have developed a range of food applicable for differing ages, including the old dog. Complete feed is the easiest and lives up to its name in that it is completely balanced – but psychologically it is disappointing be-cause it does away with the 'care' that goes into preparing the food for the dog that is dearly loved. Feeding is so sophisti-cated today that manufacturers have a prepared feed for each and every aspect of life.

The senior diet contains foods that are high in protein and lower in calories, effectively helping to build muscle and reduce weight gain, thereby relieving joint stress. Omega 3 oil is included, to help reduce joint inflammation, and glucosamine chondroitin for supple joints.

Outings and Exercise

Exercise is important to the health and wellbeing of even the elderly dog. If a canine is really finding it hard to get about, it could be worth investigating hydrotherapy/water treadmill treatment, as this maintains muscle in a non weight-bearing environment. However, this is an aerobic exercise and should only be used following veterinary referral, which your hydrotherapy centre will advise, before putting an animal at risk.

Outings are also important to the psychological wellbeing of most dogs, both young and old. Only when they are elderly and 'retired' do show dogs reach a point when they are happy to stay at home and let their younger kennel-mates rise early and enjoy the vigour of the show world. The uninformed maintain that it is cruel to take dogs to shows, but I do wish these people could see me creeping about at 4am trying to extract the dogs selected to go to the show without disturbing the others. Even in the most inclement weather, those left in their cosy beds shriek the place down because they are so furious at not being allowed to come with us to the show!

GENERAL HUSBANDRY

Cleanliness

Good husbandry and dog ownership go together equally. To behave responsibly, when a dog shares your environment, just take reasonable care. When stroking the dog and caring for his needs, make sure all wash their hands afterwards, especially children – it is children who forget these hygiene rules, then dash off to play, putting their fingers in their mouths (though it is a fact that children are more likely to get worms from other children than dogs).

Flea prevention is something to be aware off. Again take the vet's advice. He can supply a long-acting preparation, often a liquid that is put on the skin at the base of the neck. Fleas can live all year round in our modern centrally heated homes if we are not meticulous in our fight against them; though of course if the dog doesn't have fleas, then it makes your job a lot easier. The summer and autumn months are when fleas are at their most virulent.

Cleaning up when the dog goes to the toilet in the garden is obviously some-

The life cycle of a dog flea.

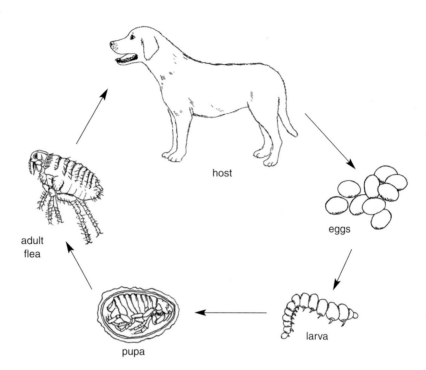

host

eggs

larva

pupa

adult flea

thing that should always be done. Poo bags are readily obtainable; they should be tied up and disposed of thoughtfully in a bin, and never just left for someone else to pick up. A supply of poo bags should be kept in the pocket of your dog-walking coat, since the responsible owner will always clean up after their dog. Many people guide their puppy to a place in the garden where the children don't go, and train their puppy to use that place. With plenty of praise and repetition this can soon be achieved, and you will benefit from having only one area to keep clean.

Vaccinations

It is important that your vet is consulted about when to vaccinate your dogs. He will also be aware of contagious diseases in your area that are preventable by vaccination. As already explained, puppies are initially given a full course, at a time when immunity from the dam has waned. Adult dogs are given boosters each year; your vet will advise when the booster is needed.

Vaccines educate the immune structure to distinguish and react to definite infections before grave illness can take hold. The vaccine has safe strains of the viruses and/or bacteria that your dog needs to be protected from: there is no cure for these diseases, so the treatment supports the immune system of the dog, hopefully helping to fight off the disease. A dog is usually vaccinated against the following conditions.

Canine distemper, or hardpad: This affects the lungs and nervous system and is usually fatal.

Infectious canine hepatitis: A virus that swiftly attacks the liver, lungs, kidneys and eyes; again, it is usually fatal.

Leptospirosis: A bacterial disease, contracted by ingesting liquid or food contaminated by the urine of rats; humans can also catch this disease. There is a second type, contracted from affected dogs' urine.

Canine parvovirus: An aggressive disease, attacking the immune system and cells lining the intestines; symptoms include severe vomiting and diarrhoea. In many cases it proves fatal, particularly in youngsters.

Dogs can also be vaccinated against canine parainfluenza, otherwise known as kennel cough, which is highly contagious. However, as with humans who are vaccinated against influenza, there are different strains so the 'cough' can still be caught. It is an airborne virus so is easily spread, particularly when many dogs are in the same area, such as at shows or in kennels.

Worming
Worms affect all dogs at some stage in life. Puppies are born with them, because they are passed on through the mother.

There are two main types of parasitic worm that affect dogs in the UK: round-

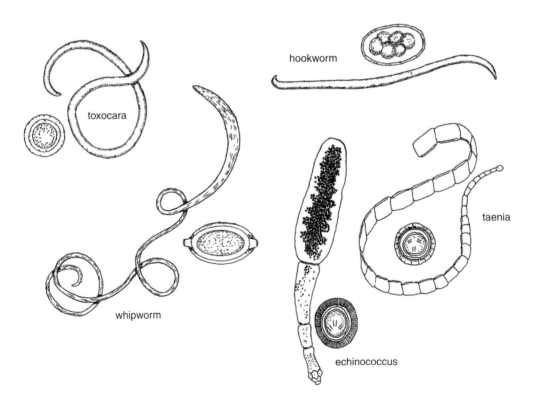

Parasitic worms and their eggs (not to scale).

worms and tapeworms. Roundworms are white and round and stretch up to 6in (15cm) in length; they resemble string. Tapeworms can grow up to 24in (60cm) in length and are flat, more similar to ribbon. The worms live in the dogs' intestines. Hookworms and whipworms also live in the intestines, but these are rare in the UK.

In Europe we seldom see parasitic worms affecting the dog's heart, lungs, bladder or stomach, although these are prevalent in some areas of America and other parts of the world. Because it is now easy for dogs to travel due to the pet passport, we should be aware of these worms.

Controlling worms in dogs is easy and successful. Your vet is the best person to consult because he can advise on products and a treatment regime. Puppies generally need worming from about two to three weeks of age until they leave for their new home; older dogs should be wormed about every six months. Like this you should have no problem with your dog having an infestation of worms. If they are not wormed with a proprietary product recommended by your vet, you run the risk of infestation, which if severe could ultimately cause poor growth, or even death in rare cases. Puppies are more likely to be seriously affected, when a large number of worms can effectively block the intestines.

Symptoms of infestation can include diarrhoea, the puppy can have a pot-bellied appearance, its coat will lack 'bloom', and it will look thin, with a protruding backbone. It may vomit up the string-like worms, and they may also be evident in the faeces. These symptoms also apply to the adult dog; another sign is a persistent cough, and the dog may rub his bottom along the floor to relieve irritation. Worms eat the contents of the dogs' intestine, which can lead to damage, and this in turn can cause bleeding.

Transmission of Worms
Roundworms eat, grow and lay eggs in the intestine of the host; these eggs are passed out in the faeces. The eggs can live in the soil for months, even years – in fact they need to stay in the environment for some time before they can infect another dog. The dog picks up the worms either by eating them from the ground, or by eating a rodent which has eaten the eggs. Immature worms can live in the tissues of infected dogs; these worms are passed to the puppy from the dam through her milk.

Tapeworms are fastened by their head to the wall of the intestine. The ribbon-like worm is made up of segments, which break off and are passed out in the faeces, resembling rice. As the dog rids himself of fleas through nibbling himself, he ingests the tapeworm. He can also eat the worm through catching and eating rabbits and rodents.

The Risk to Humans
There are horrific tales of the child being blinded by roundworms caught from the family dog: this can happen, but it is extremely rare, and it must be stressed that if a dog is competently cared for and wormed on a regular basis, it is normally unheard of.

If the human (usually a child) unfortunately became infected by roundworm, in the larval stages it would burrow through the wall of the gut, moving around the body to be embedded in, for instance, the eye. This could cause blindness.

Flea Treatment
Fleas can get everywhere, and the flea is

the most common parasite caught by the dog. Not only does their saliva cause irritation, it is also one of the most allergy-causing substances known. In severe cases, when the flea bites and draws blood it can cause anaemia.

Fleas land on the dog, bite and draw a blood meal, and mate and lay eggs, which then fall off into the surroundings. One female flea can lay 200 eggs in five days, so infestation can be truly extensive. Use of a propriety product that kills both fleas and eggs is therefore highly advisable.

There are various natural remedies that may deter the flea but will not kill it, such as garlic, citronella and brewers' yeast; however, it is best to consult your vet.

HYGIENE CONCERNS

Caring for the Coat

Obviously the character of the coat of your chosen breed will determine how much time is required to care for it. I could write at length about how to trim and prepare coats of different breeds; however, my best advice is to make an appointment with an expert in the breed, as they will know about coat texture and trimming and any idiosyncrasies pertaining to that breed.

Generally, a long-coated breed will require daily brushing, to a greater or lesser extent – so avoid a glamorously coated breed if this is not your forte. Some breeds, such as Labradors and Corgis, don't have a particularly long top coat, but do have a thick undercoat that needs regular grooming. Breeds with short coats may look easy but will still need regular grooming with a rubber 'mitt' to remove loose hair and stimulate the circulation.

Bathing too often can wash out the healthy natural oils from the coat, leaving coat and skin dry, which results in irritation so the dog is constantly scratching – a vicious circle, because he is thereby damaging the coat. In addition it reduces the insulation, so he is more likely to catch a chill. Bathing also tends to soften the coat texture, which is detrimental to breeds that need their coat to remain coarse in quality.

When bathing or showering your dog, use a shampoo that is formulated specifically for dogs. There is a huge choice of these on the market: some are antiseptic, some have the soothing properties of tea tree oil or aloe vera. However, always be sure to wash all the residue of the shampoo out, and dry your dog thoroughly, especially in the colder months.

Nail Cutting

If nails are attended to regularly when the puppy is young, the wick may stay short, so the nails will need cutting less often when the dog is an adult. It is often said that a young dog's nails will wear down naturally when he is old enough to be taken out on the hard pavement for walks; however, this is not the case. Different foot formations and the quality of the pad both influence the way in which the nail touches the floor.

Sometimes in heavy-coated breeds it is easy to forget to check the length of the nails, including the dew claw nails. It is distressing to see nails that are nearly curling back into the pad of the foot. Long nails are not only unsightly but can affect how the dog puts his foot to the floor, and may even cause splay toes.

Use clippers that have two cutting blades, rather like scissors; that way the nail is cut from both sides, not squeezing from one side (as the guillotine ones do). Battery-operated tools are also available, with an attachment that grinds; this removes the nail to the quick, with no cutting. It can be used when the dog is lying down quietly and he will soon get used to its action and will be quite relaxed about it, as he never feels pain or discomfort. If nails are clipped from a young age the dog gets used to the procedure and it does not become a battle between you and the dog.

If the nail were accidentally cut too much and bleeds, products can be readily obtained to stop the bleeding. Nails do bleed dramatically, but the dog will not bleed to death – a working dog can rip out a nail on a moor, miles from anywhere, and will survive quite happily to work another day.

Care of the Teeth

Every part of the dog is important to his wellbeing, none more so than his teeth. As with us, it is therefore important to keep the teeth healthy. Some people use a toothbrush and paste, which is fine if the dog is used to this procedure from an early age; otherwise pet food manufacturers produce chews that are specifically formulated to keep teeth healthy. Natural bones can be a contentious issue, as they can splinter. Synthetic bones, however, are ideal: they are not toxic, and chewing produces saliva. Teeth and jaw are strong and healthy as a result.

THE USE OF KENNELS

Indoor Kennels

The use of an indoor kennel/cage is without doubt a worthwhile asset. It works brilliantly as stress relief for both dog and owner, and for the owner it is a useful tool for house training. Puppy is kept in the kennel overnight or when the owners are out, so any mess can be cleaned up easily, without staining the floor covering. Upon entering the room where puppy is housed, he can be taken straight outside to relieve himself. Stay quietly with him, and when he performs, gently praise him. This says to the puppy, if he fouls his kennel he is dismissed/ignored, if he relieves himself outside he gets attention/praise. The most negative thing that can happen to a dog is to be ignored, so he soon gets the message.

It also stops any destructive behaviour. If a puppy is scolded for chewing, he is in effect gaining attention. If he is never given the opportunity to behave in this manner, it never enters his head to start.

As the puppy grows and becomes a juvenile, his actions can become very like an adolescent teenager in that he thinks he knows best. We are all creatures of habit, and benefit from routine; for example, your dog always has his morning walk at 10am, but one morning you have an appointment at this time and need to take him for his long walk at 11am – and the adolescent dog decides that this is unacceptable. If left to his own devices he would chew out of spite. However, shut in his kennel he can do nothing about his frustration while waiting for your return. Accordingly, you have confirmed your dominance in the pack, without confrontation.

From the puppy's point of view, the kennel also gives him sanctuary. Initially he will probably object to being left enclosed in it: remember he has come from an environment where he lived with his littermates. Fastened in his new kennel, in a place he doesn't recognize, probably in the dark, will leave him feeling vulnerable. A new baby would rather be snuggled up with mother, but is put in a cot for comfort and safety: likewise the puppy.

The indoor kennel serves the puppy as a cot would serve a baby. Here mum and son relax together.

To ease him into his new surroundings and kennel, you could think of leaving on a night light and a quiet radio, just so he does not feel deserted. If you really find it impossible to leave him for the first few nights, to get over the anxiety of being alone you could try putting the kennel at the side of your bed. When he cries, you can put your hand on the kennel with a few comforting words, just to settle and reassure him. But if you persist with your training and don't give in, after a few nights the puppy will see the indoor kennel as 'his place'.

Often small breeds – terriers, toys – are reared in an indoor kennel from birth so don't have any problems with it, and in fact will head off there when they are tired or stressed because it gives them security.

The kennel will give you the advantage of being able to stay with friends, or in a country cottage or caravan, accompanied by your pet. He will be secure because he has his home with him, and you will be secure in the knowledge that he will not foul or damage property that doesn't belong to you, if he is left unattended. Furthermore, when left with the freedom to wander, the puppy may not only think of chewing the chair or your favourite pair of shoes, but could find electric wires interesting.

A Place of Security

From the puppy's point of view, the kennel also gives him sanctuary and his own private space, for instance from marauding children. It lets him rest properly, which gives him the chance to grow, as all baby creatures need to do. Puppies, being inquisitive, will get up every time you do, whether it is just to pick something up from another room or to answer the phone. If he is shut in to have his nap, he will learn that he does not have to get up and down just because you do.

It must be stressed that if the indoor kennel is to fit into the new owner's lifestyle, it should be used from day one. You will not be able to put an eight-month juvenile delinquent into an indoor kennel for the first time and expect him to settle down in it: at that age he will have the strength and determination to destroy it, if he doesn't want to be there.

Our dogs are happy to live as a pack; they have plenty of room and day shelters, and sleep in draught-free, warm kennels at night.

183

Outside Kennels

Many breeders keep their dogs in outside kennels, purely because they have more dogs than comfortably fit in the home. In fact we find that our younger dogs are happier living out: they have shelter, but they also have a field to run in. Of course we interact with the dogs regularly and walk them in other places.

As they become older, they often like to live in the home, and when this happens we find they come in to live and are clean, they don't destroy possessions, and are sensible with visitors. They just learn these manners naturally, in the course of living, and never have to be taught, simply because this is how they are brought up.

Owners of one or two pet dogs can successfully have the dog in an outside kennel for part of the day. If this is your option, you must put him in the kennel for a time from day one, otherwise he is likely to object – loudly.

Remember that the garden should be protected against intruders who could steal the dog. Also the kennel must be comfortable, and sheltered from draughts, with the facility for heating in the winter months. The attached run should have an impervious floor for cleanliness, and the fencing round it should be impregnable so that the dog can neither climb up it nor tear his way out. It is wise to have the run so that he cannot see passers-by, or his owner in the house, otherwise he might bark for attention the whole time.

This option is useful for people who work shifts, because the dog is secure while they are at work and other people are at home, but they can take the dog out and give him outside stimulation when others are at work.

If the dog is to live out permanently, you should look to why you want a dog in the first place, and ask yourself if you will provide him with enough company and stimulation.

Boarding Kennels

As the owner of a boarding kennels for thirty years, we find that the dogs that settle well in boarding kennels are the ones which have been coming from a young age. They realize that their owners will return. People who never leave their dog face the prospect of one day having to leave him due to unforeseen circumstances, and the dog is then totally out of his comfort zone and can have a stressful time. This is the same scenario as never leaving your child, and then putting him in school from nine o'clock until four.

These days many boarding kennels offer a day boarding scheme, which means you can go out to work and still enjoy owning a dog: he will have the stimulation needed throughout the day, and you have the pleasure of dog ownership, without the pain of having to leave him on his own all day. Otherwise he could cause destruction and be thoroughly over-excited when you get home after your day's work.

Kennels will have opening times, but reputable establishments that offer a good service will be happy to show you the facilities during these times, without the need to make an appointment. However, it is worth bearing in mind that at peak time, during school holidays, the staff will be too busy to keep breaking off to show clients round. So please respect their commitments.

TRAINING AND COMPANIONSHIP

Housetraining

Housetraining is made easier with the use

of the indoor kennel, but the owner must still be diligent and think for the puppy. Thus each time he wakes, take him straight out, stay with him and praise him when he performs. If he stops playing and starts sniffing, again take him outside and praise him on completion. After a meal he will probably want to go out. Positive action works. If he has an accident in the house, ignore him, and put it down to you not thinking quickly enough.

Some breeds are easy to housetrain. Smaller breeds seem to be harder to train, though perhaps this is because we are not as vigilant because they don't cause much mess. For example, we have a small terrier dog: at ten weeks old he was totally housetrained, a bright little dog. By fifteen weeks, however, he had learned to cock his leg – we would find a puddle at the table leg or the edge of an open door, but I never caught him in the act, and he was so sure of himself that I am quite sure he did this, as a terrier would, just to prove he could! As Stephen says, 'Gundogs live to please you, terriers live to please themselves!'

Travel Training

The journey home with his new owner is probably the first time in a car for the puppy, so on this occasion he can perhaps be cuddled on someone's knee. After that, however, it is important to make a safe place for him, perhaps in a crate in the back of the car or behind a dog guard. If he cries, reassure him, but don't give him too much attention or he will think disruptive behaviour is always rewarded.

Don't let the dog loose in the car, and don't let him sit on your knee whilst you are driving – these are both potentially dangerous habits.

Playing Games

Puppies need stimulation, and playing is a fun way of learning. However, don't let games get out of hand or the puppy will start snapping, which as he gets older could lead to biting. It is natural for a young dog to use his teeth to play – you only have to watch siblings in the nest. It is not acceptable, however, for the puppy to snap at humans, so this must be discouraged, and if he gets overexcited in play, give him his toy to pull on, rather than you, and calm the proceedings down.

As the dog grows, if he is getting overexcited in play, he may start to 'hump'. At this stage this is not a sexual issue, but again, give him something else to think of, so that he does not grow up hanging on to visitors' legs. This behaviour can lead to the 'humping' becoming a dominance issue, so it must be stopped.

Socializing with Other Dogs and Livestock

Instinct, and a lack of useful stimulus and/or training, can lead most breeds to be unsociable and dangerous to livestock. Nevertheless, many breeds can be taught to stay close to you when approaching other dogs or walking through fields of sheep, and it is a good idea to establish this training whilst the puppy is young and still feeling vulnerable, and therefore more likely to stay near to you.

Often one hears that the dog was bitten whilst young: 'He just went to say hello, but as he approached the dog bit him, and now he is aggressive to other dogs.' But to allow your dog to run up to a strange dog quite freely is asking for trouble: you wouldn't dash up to a stranger and throw your arms around them, and if you did, you would probably be strongly rebuked! Have a quiet word

As siblings reach adolescence, the play fights could become more serious.

with passing dog walkers, and ask if they would be happy for their dog to play with your youngster. And if the breed you have is more likely to follow his instinct and rush off, rather than obeying your call or whistle, then it would be sensible to take him out on a retractable lead.

It is worth noting that it is probably not wise to walk through a field of cows with their calves, even if there is a footpath. Cows are very protective of their young and will charge a dog.

Most breeds, even terriers, can be taught to live in harmony with cats or pet rabbits or the like, if introduced to them early enough. However, be aware that a cat could injure an inquisitive puppy by scratching his face or eyes.

Coping with Two Dogs

Many people say they want two dogs. Well, two puppies at the same time might work with some of the smaller breeds, but generally you just have 'double trouble'.

How do you train two puppies? Whilst you are involved with one, the other is vying for attention – even if you dismiss the second puppy, it is still actually getting your time as you send it away. If you fasten one up to play with the other, it will object loudly.

Similarly, lead training two puppies does not work, because they simply become competitive about it. Having two, with the thought that they will occupy each other when you are away from the home, could result in their causing devastation: one puppy might just chew the corner of a cushion, but two will tear it apart – great 'game'. Who is to be scolded? You have no idea who caused the trouble.

Two dogs living together can be a positive feature, but they need to be different ages. If one dog is trained and well behaved when you decide on having a second, the older dog will have the effect of teaching good behaviour to the young newcomer. However, if you feel that having another dog is a good way to occupy a badly behaved older dog, then you will not find it easy.

If you feel you would like a second dog and would like to give a 'rescue' dog a good home, think carefully. An older dog may not fit in with a peer, as they could have issues as to who is to be top dog. If you choose to have another dog of the same sex, you could encounter peer pressure as they age. A puppy will look up to the older one, but when the youngster reaches adolescence he may take on the older dog for a higher position in the pecking order, especially if both are males.

If both are females, they could fall out when the hormones start raging when they are coming into season – and this may happen nine weeks after the season when the bitch 'thinks' she is having puppies and becomes protective.

A positive rationale is to have both dogs neutered, which should solve any potential problems. Neutering also precludes medical problems in later life, such as prostate problems in males and womb infections in bitches.

CONCLUSION

Throughout this book we have drawn on the experiences that we have had through our years of dog breeding.

We started showing dogs as a result of a competitive streak developed by competing in other country activities and skills, such as 'Young Farmers' club activities and showing stock animals at country shows. The showing of dogs led naturally to breeding – as it does with most reputable dog breeders.

In our passion for our chosen breed, our aim is, and has always been, to produce healthy, contented dogs that conform to the standard laid down for the breed, whilst retaining their inherent instinct, which makes them what they are and provides them with the stimulation so they remain fulfilled.

Respect, for us, is the most important word in the language. When breeding dogs, we must respect nature, as she will always have the final say. We must also have respect for what we are doing, enhancing and ensuring a sound future for the breed we love. Furthermore the dogs produced by us should be placed in homes where the individuals have our respect and honesty, combined with knowledgeable support from us. It is so rewarding to hear from an owner saying that the dog they have had as part of their lives for the last fourteen or so years, has given so much to the family – the best thing they ever did.

Because of our relative lifespans we have dogs for such a short time, but they give so much, and leave such memories when they are gone. What creature, other than the dog, has that ability? He truly deserves our respect.

We have been constantly uplifted by our peers who have such a passion for their breeds. They have given us a share in their history through their photographs and pedigrees, and we hope that many will glean sound knowledge from these and from this book for many years to come.

The authors with their dogs.

FURTHER INFORMATION

FURTHER READING

Clark, Anne R., and Brace, Andrew H. (eds), *The International Encyclopaedia of Dogs* (Howell Book House Inc, New York, 1995)

Kane, Frank, *Judging the Gundog Breeds* (Ibex Web Solutions, 2009)

The Kennel Club Illustrated Breed Standard (Ebury Press, London, 2011)

Willis, Dr Malcolm B., *Genetics of the Dog* (H.F & G. Witherby Ltd, London, 1989)

USEFUL WEBSITES

The Kennel Club
www.thekennelclub.org.uk

The Young Kennel Club
www.ykc.org.uk

The following are a selection of the many breed associations that can be contacted via the internet. Space does not allow for every breed mentioned in this book, but this constitutes a representative selection. Most websites contain links to other breed associations throughout the world.

Hound Breeds
The Afghan Hound Association
www.ahaonline.co.uk

The Basset Hound Club
www.bassethoundclub.co.uk

The Beagle Association
www.beagleassociation.org.uk

The Irish Wolfhound Club
www.irishwolfhoundclub.org.uk

The Miniature Dachshund Club
www.miniaturedachshundclub.co.uk

Gundog Breeds
The English Setter Association
www.englishsetterassociation.co.uk

The Gordon Setter Association
www.gordon-setter-association.co.uk

The Irish Setter Association
www.isae.co.uk

Retriever Breeds
The Clumber Spaniel Club
www.clumberspanielclub.co.uk

The Cocker Spaniel Club
www.thecockerspanielclub.co.uk

The Labrador Retriever Club
www.thelabradorretrieverclub.com

Hunt, Point, Retrieve Breeds
The Hungarian Vizsla Society
www.vizsla.org.uk

The Weimaraner Association
www.weimaraner-association.org.uk

Terrier Breeds
The Bull Terrier Club
www.thebullterrierclub.com

The Cairn Terrier Club
www.thecairnterrierclub.co.uk

National Airedale Terrier Association
www.nationalairedale.co.uk

The Staffordshire Bull Terrier Club
www.thesbtc.com

Utility Breeds
The British Bulldog Club
www.britishbulldogclub.co.uk

The British Dalmatian Club
www.britishdalmatianclub.org.uk

The Schnauzer Club of Great Britain
www.schnauzerclub.co.uk

Working Breeds
Alaskan Malamute Working Association
www.amwa.co.uk

The UK Dobermann Association
www.ukdobermannassociation.com

The Mastiff Association
www.mastiffassociation.com

The Newfoundland Dog Club
www.thenewfoundlandclub.co.uk

The Siberian Husky Club
www.siberianhuskyclub.com

Pastoral Breeds
The Border Collie Club
www.bordercollieclub.com

The Briard Association
www.briard-association.co.uk

The German Shepherd Dog League
www.gsdleague.co.uk

The Samoyed Association
www.thesamoyedassociation.co.uk

The Cardigan Welsh Corgi Association
www.cardiganwelshcorgiassoc.co.uk

Toy Breeds
The Affenpinscher Club
www.affenpinscherclubuk.com

The British Chihuahua Club
www.the-british-chihuahua-club.org.uk

The Papillon Club
www.papillonclub.co.uk

The Yorkshire Terrier Club
www.the-yorkshire-terrier-club.co.uk

INDEX